The Love of God
and The Age to Come

The Love of God
and The Age to Come

No Eternal Hell

By THOMAS RONALD VAUGHAN

WIPF & STOCK · Eugene, Oregon

THE LOVE OF GOD AND THE AGE TO COME
No Eternal Hell

Copyright © 2019 Thomas Ronald Vaughan. All rights reserved. Except for brief quotations in critical publications or reviews, no part of this book may be reproduced in any manner without prior written permission from the publisher. Write: Permissions, Wipf and Stock Publishers, 199 W. 8th Ave., Suite 3, Eugene, OR 97401.

Wipf & Stock
An Imprint of Wipf and Stock Publishers
199 W. 8th Ave., Suite 3
Eugene, OR 97401

www.wipfandstock.com

PAPERBACK ISBN: 978-1-5326-7944-5
HARDCOVER ISBN: 978-1-5326-7945-2
EBOOK ISBN: 978-1-5326-7946-9

Manufactured in the U.S.A.   03/20/19

This book is dedicated to the memory of Charles K. Robinson, professor of theology at the Divinity School of Duke University. He published few articles; he never wrote a book. But, he stood behind a lectern, year after year, telling class after class that God loved everyone who ever lived and that that love would not let us go in time or eternity.

Now he knows. . . .

"I, the Lord, am the maker of all things."
—Isaiah 44:24

"For from him and through him and to him are all things."
—Romans 11: 36

"God is love."
—I John 4:8

"Nothing can separate us from God's love."
—Romans 8:39

"God creates a succession of worlds."
—Origen

"He descended into hell."
—The Apostles Creed

"Hell is God's Hell."
—The author

"All shall be well, and all shall be well,
and all manner of thing shall be well."
—Julian of Norwich

Contents

Preface | xi

PART ONE ... in which I introduce the issues

The Unpardonable Sin of Western Theology | 3

What Is God Doing Today? | 6
    Footnote: Conditional Immortality | 7

Progression to Perfection | 9

Eternal Hell Preaches Well | 11

Thirteen Hell-Inspired Questions | 14

Six Premises | 17
    Footnote: Defining Agape | 19

Why This Book | 21

Hell and God's Character | 25

Who Is This God? | 27

Because God Says So | 30

God Is Responsible | 35

PART TWO . . . in which I turn to the Bible

Inspired, Inerrant, Infallible? | 41

We Cannot Do "Biblical Theology" | 46

How To Write A Gospel | 50

Just A Little Help | 53

Saying "Hell" In The Gospels | 57

John's Gospel: Based On A True Story | 60

Paul: Hell Yes; Hell No | 67
    1. First and Second Thessalonians | 69
    2. Romans | 70

More Pauline Universalism | 74
    1. 1 Corinthians and 2 Corinthians | 74
    2. Galatians | 76
    3. Philippians | 76
    4. Colossians | 77

Six Universalist Writings | 79
    1. James | 79
    2. The Pastoral Epistles | 80
    3. First and Second Peter | 81
    4. Ephesians | 82

No Hell In Acts | 84

The Minority: Eternal Hell | 86

Jesus Did Not Teach Eternal Hell | 92
    Footnote: Luke 6:43–45 | 99
    Footnote: Comments on Matthew 24, Luke 21,
        and Mark 13 | 103
    Footnote: Matthew 24:51 | 104

    Footnote: The Thief On The Cross (Luke 23:43) | 110
    Footnote: The Sin Against The Holy Spirit | 111
    Footnote: The Rich Man and Lazarus | 113
    Footnote: Why Bother If We Cannot Know? | 114

PART THREE . . . in which I redefine Hell

We All Go To Hell | 119

Hell Is God's Hell | 121

    Footnote: Eternal Forgiveness | 123

What In Hell Is Going On?
Resistance and Renewal | 125

What In Hell Is Going On?
Forgiveness and Reconciliation | 128

Soft On Sin? | 132

The True Harrowing Of Hell | 134

Conclusion | 137

Where To Go From Here | 139

Preface

THIS IS A BOOK of essays written around a common theme. I use a "building block" approach to present this theme, but each essay can stand on its own. Since this is true, I may be forgiven repeating or restating some material in order to make separate essays intelligible. I have tried to keep excessive redundancy to a bare minimum and I believe I have succeeded.

I have no interest in writing philosophy, but rather philosophical theology, if I may be allowed the term. The theology is squarely within the liberal Judeo Christian Biblical tradition. My approach to the text is historical – critical. Several essays are on the subject of scripture interpretation. Everything I propose, even as I freely speculate here, has a Biblical referent which allows me to say what I do. I view this as being Biblically conservative even while using higher and lower criticism to interpret the text. I note that I sprinkle footnotes here and there to comment upon topics not entirely germane to my overall focus.

I can name the year, if not the date, that I became a convinced and convicted universalist. It was 1969. I have, therefore, been thinking about all of this for quite a while. That is no commendation for its truthfulness or correctness, so much as it is a testimony to how this faith has buoyed me through the vicissitudes of my own life. I have tried to view my world, and the world around me, through the lens of belief that God will save everyone. It has made all the difference in both these "worlds."

Preface

If Kierkegaard is right that "truth is subjectivity," then universal redemption is truth for me. However, since God is "agape love," and will indeed save us all, universalism is true independent of whether I, or anyone else, believes it.

I affirm that God will save us all. I deny the existence of an eternal hell. The following essays present my reasons.

PART ONE

...in which I introduce the issues

The Unpardonable Sin of Western Theology

The "Satisfaction Theory of Atonement" has held sway in western thought for over 1500 years. It was the dominant view in Roman Catholicism, and swept unnoticed and without objection into the several theological streams of its stepchild, the Protestant Reformation. Its staying power is attested to by the fact that it is the foundational doctrine for Roman Catholicism and much of Protestantism to this present day. Nevertheless, it is totally flawed in its major tenets and features. I call it boldly an unpardonable theological sin.

The Satisfaction Theory is built on a definition and understanding of God which is not Biblical and is certainly false. It presents a God who has, in non-theological language, two sides to her personality. One is kind, gentle, benevolent, and loving. The other is wrathful, angry, and punishing. And then enters the human race, created by God, which proceeds, every member, to fall into sin. God has loved the human race, but in its descent into sin, God's rage is kindled. That is, in short, the dilemma, for both God and humanity, which the Satisfaction Theory of Atonement addresses and claims to resolve. It does not.

It does not resolve this problem for the simple reason that there is no problem to resolve. It is a pseudo-problem based on erroneous assumptions.

The theory goes on to declare that in order to appease the anger of God, an acceptable sacrifice, an atonement, must be

PART ONE . . . in which I introduce the issues

provided. In the Old Testament this was a monumental problem, for no "perfect sacrifice" was to be found. Luckily, however, for the human race, God himself intervened, and in the first century provided that perfect sacrifice in the person of Jesus of Nazareth.

The best language describing this situation is both legal and accounting. In the balance sheet of their sins, all sinners fell woefully short. They, of course, could not save themselves. They were hopelessly guilty as transgressors. They were doomed. The only rightful "sentence" for these wretches was, of course, consignment to a proper place of punishment and retribution. God had conveniently created such a place, a fiery, eternal hell, which he deemed the appropriate environment for these law-breakers who had tarnished and besmirched his dignity, and flouted his merciful justice.

There was, thankfully, a way to dispel God's rage and come back into the saving graces and loving embrace. That way was simple: accept in humility and heartfelt repentance the beneficent provision offered through the atoning one, Jesus. How sinners were to "accept" Jesus, and thus benefit from his and now God's atonement, was a subject of much discussion and debate among the many groups who espoused the Theory. How, in fact, Jesus did anything to actually atone for sin and thereby re-categorize sinners from lost to saved was also never satisfactorily addressed. The simplistic version seems to be that God himself did the accounting by accepting the sinner's acceptance of Jesus and then declaring the wayward one "not guilty!" It was a most fascinating and breathtaking Creation-in-thought, and a curious mythology about God and eternal intentions.

The fact of the matter is this: there is not one verse in scripture that describes God as conflicted internally between love and wrath. There is not one verse in scripture that declares that God needs a second party, an intermediary, to resolve the conflict. There is not one verse in the New Testament in which Jesus describes his role as abating the rage of God toward sinners. There is not one verse that portrays God's wrath as anything but situationally reactive to human sin. There is not a single verse that concludes that God's

The Unpardonable Sin of Western Theology

anger and love are eternally bifurcated, which would absolutely be required for God to be loving and kind toward those in heaven, and wrathful and angry toward those in hell.

Much of the content of these essays attempts to define the character of God. I desire to reclaim that character from those who attribute to her such outrageous assertions as that she has created and currently sustains an environment in which millions of her creatures reside in horrors, pain, and suffering, and that thousands more are hourly joining them.

I also propose that theology should turn a new focus upon Jesus.

As I state in my closing essay, "Where to go from here?," the entire subject-doctrine of the person and work of Jesus of Nazareth must be revisited. What, indeed, do the terms "atonement" and "sacrifice" mean when applied to Jesus? What does he mean when he utters these, or similar, words? I affirm that only through the lens of agapeistic universalism can answers be given which are true to God's eternally formulated intentions and actions in human history. It is, historically, time for "The Satisfaction Theory of Atonement" to be discarded in favor of more Biblically correct views of God, Jesus, and issues of eternal life. God is not waffling between love and wrath.

The love of God is inclusive, indiscriminate, and everlasting. It does not require an intermediary, atonement, or any substitutionary sacrifice in order to lavish purifying and redeeming grace upon all humanity, in any world, and for all eternity.

My objections to this pervasive theological system must be kept firmly in mind when reading the essays in this book.

What Is God Doing Today?

THEOLOGY GETS IT INTERPRETIVE bearings by looking back. It makes its prophetic forecasts by looking forward. It is, however, notoriously unable to give definitive interpretations and explanations for what is occurring in the present moment. I am, of course, speaking of theology assessing events in human history.

However, there is a realm of the present to which theology can speak—if it dare—and that quite definitely. It is in the matter of what God is doing vis-à-vis those who have died to enter life "beyond the grave." I heard a very famous minister say recently that there are "millions of people in eternal hell right now." It sounds as if he has a strong opinion about what God is actually doing today.

His is the position I am objecting to here. It must affirm that God is in his heaven, overseeing the affairs of those residing there, overseeing the affairs of the world, and at the same time, overseeing the most horrific scene of which the human mind is capable of imagining. God is, either directly or indirectly, orchestrating the suffering, pain, and anguish of untold millions who have been consigned to that infernal place. They are there by the direct action of God herself, who daily watches as thousands more plunge to such a fate. That is precisely what God is doing in this present hour, according those who believe in unending torment in a fiery hell.

There is, however, another position. It affirms that God is in his heaven, overseeing that realm, and is also interfacing with affairs on earth in a mysterious way. But at the same time God is

What Is God Doing Today?

maintaining in "soul sleep" all the dead. They will be roused on a second advent of Jesus the Christ, at which time their eternal fate will be determined. Righteous persons will be allowed into heaven with God. Unrighteous persons will be annihilated, to be extinct forevermore. These are the things God is doing now.

I endorse another option. God is in his heaven, overseeing the welfare of those abiding there, as well as mysteriously interacting in the affairs of the world. But God is doing something entirely different with those who have not yet entered heaven. God is lovingly directing and guiding them through her carefully designed contexts which produce the final outcome of eternal life in her holy realm. This action is undertaken and ultimately completed for everyone, and that forever. That is what God is doing, even in this moment.

While we have no ability to know everything God is doing, we cannot be mistaken in asserting that in this very delimited area of God's activity, something much like this must be going on now. If I am correct, then these conclusions are quite unavoidable. There are three radically different systems of Christian theology operating here. There are, accordingly, three fundamentally different Gods (or gods) actively at work now.

Footnote: Conditional Immortality

This is a position in Christian theology that speaks in an unique way to the issue of life after death. It had adherents in Christian antiquity, and is believed by many today. It has been a minor undercurrent of thought throughout history.

The condition which must be met in order for one to achieve eternal life in God's heaven is righteousness and faithfulness. Those who lack these qualities are not sent to hell; they are simply annihilated and destroyed forever. They do not exist after God's action to cast them into the Lake of Fire, as it is called in Revelation 20. They die an eternal death. God (who else?) kills them!

While this view does remove the onus on God for creating and perpetuating an everlasting punishing hell, it diminishes

PART ONE . . . in which I introduce the issues

considerably the definition of agape love. God may have the power and wisdom to reclaim sinners, even into eternity, but God apparently does not love them enough to do so.

This theology turns on ideas about the second advent of Jesus Christ, at which time everyone will be examined regarding their status for eternity.

For God to simply destroy evil people is minimally to declare a divine failure of cosmic proportions. That is not acceptable to any reader of the New Testament or any student of the life of Jesus. I will reference this view only in passing throughout. I am primarily speaking here to those advocating an eternity of "fire and brimstone." But surely conditional immortality does indeed tarnish the reputation and character of the God it represents.

Progression to Perfection

MUCH OF MY THEOLOGY of life in the age to come turns on the notion of "progression to perfection." I maintain categorically that such a concept is completely Biblical, and is essential for understanding what God requires from each of us. I write on this from the beginning page of these essays, but I will here outline the core ingredients in the concept.

Progressive "sanctification" is an ancient Christian term indicating the process, in this earthly life, whereby a Christian after conversion grows in grace toward a rather vaguely defined spiritual "maturity." It is a relational undertaking between the individual and God, whereby God bestows transforming grace on her children. The goal, as Paul says in Philippians 1:6, is this: ". . . that God, who began a good work in you, will carry it on to completion. . ." Later in the same book Paul declares that he himself has not fully matured, but through God's grace he presses, he progresses on "toward the goal to win the prize. . . for which God has called me heavenward in Christ Jesus" (3:14). The vectors of progress are not always straight, however. In Romans, Paul laments his ongoing sin and sinfulness, asking, "Who will deliver me?" (Romans 7:24). His answer is, "Jesus Christ" (verse 25).

Several other New Testament verses make the same point, and teach the mandated requirement that Christians grow, mature, and develop, as they aspire for holiness in a lifestyle pleasing to God. Their effort is nothing less than a grateful response to God's goodness toward us, and is also acknowledgement of the benefits

PART ONE . . . in which I introduce the issues

and merits of the life and work of Jesus Christ. It is a wholly praiseful act toward God.

Few would disagree with the obligatory Christian command to grow in grace. But due to the constraints of their theology, most would have little to say about how the doctrine relates to individuals at the time of their deaths, and thereafter. Where I reside, a common sentence in newspaper obituaries is a perfect example of this theology. Daily stories of deaths locally often include the name of the deceased followed by, ". . .went home to be with the Lord." The message is clear that the person went immediately to God's heavenly abode.

I ask here, as I will again, "Is anyone perfect, mature, and holy at death?" I am certain that the answer to my query is, "No!," as I am certain that God, nevertheless demands it. Did Jesus believe in human perfectibility before death? Did Paul, or anyone else in the early Christian church, believe they would achieve spiritual perfection before physical death? Many early Christians believed in the imminent return of Jesus Christ. Did they presume that any would be holy and ready for that event?

All serious Christian theology must agree that God will not allow the contaminating effect of human sin into her holy presence. She must, therefore, graciously provide other intermediate contexts wherein all are shepherded through a progression to perfection. If it is not so, none will ever see heaven.

I will attempt to flesh out this concept in the pages that follow. My conclusions are speculative, but supported by Biblical references throughout. We know very little about life in the age to come, but since Christian faith affirms its eventual reality for everyone, it seems that the same faith gives us permission to think carefully about it.

Eternal Hell Preaches Well

CONTEMPORARY MESSAGING FROM OUR fundamentalist and evangelical platforms often portrays God and Jesus as distraught or in tears, as souls reject the offer of salvation and descend into unending hell. This sensational portrayal is highly offensive to anyone who has contemplated the love of God and the heart of Jesus. It is crassly devious and deceptive, since the sad and weeping deities are themselves the "owners and operators" of the hell into which these human souls drop—and that on order from the deities!

It is beyond fraudulent to imply that these all-powerful divinities are now simply powerless to do anything other than to painfully watch. It is disingenuous to hold up a representation of any God who cares deeply when "one sparrow falls" (Mt. 10:29), but who does nothing at all to assist or intervene for the unfortunate God-created human beings (not birds) who plummet into the ghastly nether regions.

Some of the world's most famous preachers have asserted in the past, and do so powerfully today, that "God loves you!" When in truth they mean this: God loves you until you die, at which time he will cast you into a flaming hell forever, if you have not done several things which the preaching minister can most certainly enumerate for you! That preaching often begins with the spine-straightening question: "Do you know where you will spend eternity?" The more honest question would be: "Do you know what to do to keep God from casting you into eternal fire and torment?" Likely, the audience will not hear that!

PART ONE . . . in which I introduce the issues

Thousands of such sermons are preached weekly, heard by tens of thousands of auditors, who seem determined and contented to believe the message, endorse the theology, and praise the preaching as true to God's word, and furthermore, to God's character and intentions.

The story of "how we got here" can be told by another more qualified to do it. We have been here for well over a hundred years, at least in the many fundamentalist-evangelical churches. In our times, this approach to "soul winning" has evolved into a massive institutional and media mega-industry. It has produced superstar personalities, selling millions of books, tapes, videos, even coffee mugs and t-shirts! It fills "churches" with tens of thousands of financially contributing worshippers. It has merchandized its "gospel" in ways that would make an MBA or a Wall Street banker proud of the bottom line numbers. And, of course, it can point to huge quantities of nameless "souls" it has snatched from the pit of hell.

Ought anyone be brazen and audacious enough to criticize this "Christian enterprise" which clearly does some marvelous good despite its embarrassing financial and celebrity excesses? Ought I to write that "Preaching Hell Sells Well?" Yes, of course, someone can and should observe and comment where there is one hundred and eighty degrees of disagreement between the message preached and the message that ought to be preached!

I have a long list of concerns, which grew longer during my years in parish ministry. My main difficulties, however, were and are not with personalities, institutions, programs, and budgets—though I have some grave concerns here—so much as they are with the Biblical theological foundations upon which this monstrous edifice is built. I offer strong objections to the doctrine of unending torment and to the fundamentalist view of the Bible which preserves it. These are the two foundation stones for this spiritual structure, and I am quite certain that both are pernicious and most unhealthy for all things Christian. I am equally certain that Christianity, once freed from these strongly bound chains, can present itself afresh to a world in desperate need of its grace-filled message of redemption, renewal, and hope.

Fundamentalists demand the best from the modern age in all areas, from technology to media to transportation and architecture. Yet, they obstinately resist all resources of modern scholarship when it comes to studying scripture. If the Bible can be loosed from this fundamentalist stranglehold, and if the fires of an eternal hell are finally extinguished, Christians can joyfully rediscover, in our time, the true character of the God of love, the son of that love, and the unleashed power of a new spirit at work in the world. The doctrine of universalism is the new paradigm. Through it, all of doctrinal Christianity can be rethought, reformulated, and reintroduced to every person and culture on earth.

I believe it is high time for fundamentalists to drop fundamentalism and to redefine evangelism more in line with the eternal intentions of agape love. I have no doubt that the heart of fundamentalism-evangelicalism is in the right place. The head is not. Would it not be world changing for its exhorters to stand and proclaim that "God loves you!" without the threat of unending doom attached to the message?

Throughout the long history of the human race, countless millions of parents have told their children, with depthless sincerity, that they could do nothing—absolutely nothing—that would extinguish parental love. Sad to relate that a doctrine of fundamentalist-evangelical Christianity puts that heartfelt reality to a shattering lie, for it teaches that God Almighty will not love and do the acts of love for millions of his children, but will condemn them to a frightening pain-filled hell forevermore!

Why would not such Christians rejoice to think that modern methods of Biblical scholarship and interpretation could offer them a chance to believe in, and teach, the eternal triumph of love through the kindness and generosity of the God of all creation?

Thirteen Hell-Inspired Questions

MOST CHRISTIANS HAVE LITTLE interest in, or desire to investigate, eternal hell or to ponder the shocking reality of the millions assumed to be there now, or who are surely "on their way." But when this doctrine is a major tenet of one's basic theology, and it involves the final "resting" place of real live known or unknown human creatures, one might do well to make some room for reflective consideration of this cherished belief.

Tens of million believe it, but give it almost no thought whatsoever. The following questions force that thought, but in a gentle way. They present some queries that can frame this topic for that thoughtful reflection. These are questions that I think must be included in honest deliberations on God and a doctrine of eternal hell. Here, I use the term, "hell," for the New Testament Greek word, Gehenna, and for the term as used in common parlance among proponents of the doctrine. I will, however, radically redefine it as these essays progress.

Question 1: Eternal hell is a dominant teaching in much of Christian theology. Why are there no scriptural references to its creation by God?

Question 2: Since God is omniscient, all-knowing and wise, did she not know that most people would reject all "saving offers," and upon their deaths go to this hellish place she had created?

Thirteen Hell-Inspired Questions

Question 3: Since nothing is self-sustaining but God, who, but God, is now sustaining both the existence of hell and all who are consigned there?

Question 4: God is love. Does God love for all eternity those he sends to hell? What does that even mean?

Question 5: God has desired that "none should perish." Does God abandon that desire when a soul falls into hell?

Question 6: Is a human free will decision to reject God's "saving offers" more powerful than God's will, desire, and love to "save" that human?

Question 7: God self-defines in scripture as a Mother-Father who deeply loves her children. Can any parent subject a loved, cherished, and prized child to an eternity of unending misery?

Question 8: Will redeemed souls in heaven know their loved ones are in the anguish and pain of hell?

Question 9: Since, at death, none are "ready" for God's holy presence, how does God prepare them for that presence?

Question 10: If hell is eternal, will there not also be an eternal duality? Is this an acceptable interpretation of God's plan to be "all in all?"

Question 11: If God is impassive toward eternal suffering, what are followers to make of Bible teaching to "do good" to those in need, want, hunger, or pain?

Question 12: What attribute or characteristic of God does the living reality of hell celebrate, vindicate, or "satisfy?"

Question 13: Finally, what if, in fact, hell and all its ramparts have a time-delimited existence known only to God? What if hell does exist, is not eternal, but is rather a complex context designed solely to accomplish the saving goals of agape love?

I quite clearly understand that mere mortals cannot answer definitively and exhaustively many of these questions. They are here to stimulate deep thought upon long-held beliefs about the

PART ONE . . . in which I introduce the issues

very character of God Almighty and God's plans for final realities. I have deemed them a helpful bridge into the material included in upcoming essays. They, at least, place before us many mental images, ideas, and concepts that naturally arise in such an unusual study as this. They can focus thinking for our best effort.

I am not a fount of all wisdom, but I will attempt to comment upon these questions, giving the best information I can to assist in answers, even if some of those answers are necessarily incomplete. That information is scattered here and there throughout these pages.

The book title implies another question: Is it possible that God will eventually save everyone? The title itself gives the stirring answer: Yes! God will save us all!

Six Premises

THIS BOOK IS BASED on six premises. They are dealt with directly in six essays, and indirectly in all the remaining pages. The format is simply to elucidate the implications or corollaries from the premises. For example, if God is a God of agape love for all her creatures, she could not, by the definition of agape, damn just one of them to unending torment and suffering. And each premise is likewise fleshed out and enlarged upon throughout. Here are the six premises.

1. The predominant characteristic or attribute of the Lord God Almighty is agape love. This loving God will not allow any of his children to suffer eternal torment.
2. Accordingly, as the "Son" of this God, Jesus of Nazareth did not teach unending torment, but eternal salvation for all.
3. The Apostle Paul taught eternal damnation early in his career, but became "persuaded" of the power of God's love, and taught universal redemption thereafter.
4. Of the remaining books in the New Testament, the majority teach universal salvation.
5. Of the remaining books in the New Testament, a minority teach eternal torment.
6. God accomplishes universal redemption by creating contexts and environments, in the age to come, through which all persons progress toward perfect holiness.

PART ONE . . . in which I introduce the issues

I purposely refrain from using the word, "Purgatory," for the concept I am presenting here. It is not the term for what I propose. While I have no problem with the adjective, "purgatorial," and its implied rehabilitative and redemptive action, I will not use it either. "Purgatory" as a place for the dead, belongs to the theology of a particular branch of Christianity, and is associated with a hierarchical human organization teaching a meritorious, legal system of salvation (see the first essay). With that system I share no affinity. These terms are, therefore, best avoided here, I believe.

Hell, admittedly, is an unfortunate term, but it is continuously used in religious circles to reference an infernal, punishing, and eternal environment. I have determined not to create a new term, but rather to redefine hell, giving it its proper redemptive function.

It should go without saying that any human being who is alive after his or her physical death will have been given that life by a Higher Power. Neither science nor religion has convincingly demonstrated that life after death is a natural characteristic of the human species.

Christians are not the only religious people who have believed in life after death. However, many Christians find themselves in the extremely uncomfortable position of affirming that this Higher Power—called God—will give this life to untold multitudes of the deceased only to then cast them into a place of pain, suffering, and misery forever. This fact raises serious questions about the moral character and intentions of a God who would orchestrate such a shocking outcome for, as many teach, millions, even billions, of souls.

However, in Christian thought there is, thankfully, an alternative view to the above macabre horror story. It is far more optimistic and encouraging, for it declares that God, the Higher Power, does indeed bestow life on the deceased, but that this God desires an eternal relationship with every creature she has created. In fact, that is why they were created—to eventually come to love God and enjoy him forever in the glorious company of everyone who has ever lived.

Six Premises

In this book I will be openly declaring the truth of this latter position, and will argue against any other position, with special attention to the outrageous idea that a so-called "God of Love" could actually consign millions of her creatures to fruitless torment in a hell that must be of God's own creation and continuing control.

I will rightly look to the New Testament as the origin of both the doctrine of eternal hell and of universal salvation. I will ask, "What did the Apostle Paul teach?" I will ask, "What is the teaching of the rest of the New Testament?" And most importantly, I will inquire, "What did Jesus teach?" Several other pertinent topics are addressed as I attempt to present my own ideas and concepts related to a new definition of the purposes and scope of "hell."

To answer these Biblical questions, I will rely upon the methods of higher criticism in interpretation. This is in direct opposition to fundamentalist approaches to the text. I speak to this contrast throughout these essays.

This book proclaims that God will save us all because God's predominant attribute is called in Greek, agape love. It is the highest form of love imaginable, and is powerful and determined enough to secure the salvation of all persons.

Can this love save all? Will this love save all? I answer in the affirmative: Yes, God's love is out for nothing less than ultimate universal redemption.

Footnote: Defining Agape

Ancient and Koine (New Testament) Greek offer several words which the much poorer English language translates, "love." By common consent among scholars, agape is the highest form of love, originating in the "heart" of God, and is showered on his human race. John 3:16, "For God so loved the world...," and I John 4:8,16, "God is love...," use the term. If, in fact, it is love originating in God, human definitions and understandings are decidedly limited, and limiting. As an attribute of God, this love can be as little fathomed as any divine attribute, such as power, wisdom or immortality. This is a very important point since many Christian theologies are quite

PART ONE . . . in which I introduce the issues

sure that God's saving agape love cannot extend to life after death for the "unsaved" and "unrighteous." Even as that is proclaimed to be true, humans can never know the extent of God's beneficence toward the living or the dead. Universalism alone is comfortable declaring that agape will unquestionably extend beyond death, for all creatures, and will accomplish its saving purposes. There are no theological grounds for declaring a limit, in time or eternity, to the effectual working of this love. To imply that God loves sinners, with agape love, until the moment they die in an unrepentant state, is anathema. And to go further and announce that thereafter God casts them into an eternal flaming inferno called hell, is scandalous. Additionally, to state that God loves, with agape love, those roiling in the confines of a fiery doom, is to construct a sentence which has no logical cohesion whatsoever.

Universalism acknowledges the depthlessness of this love, even as it focuses on two of its characteristics. Agape love is unconditional, and it always acts in the best interest of the beloved.

"Unconditional" simply means the absence of conditions that must be met in order for God to love. It speaks to sinful acts of human creatures as well. Even those who believe in eternal hell proclaim that this love extends to the rankest sinner in this life, and that it waits in hope for the sinner to acknowledge the sin and turn from it. Then, there is unanimous agreement on the meaning of the term unconditional, even as there is unanimous disagreement on whether God's loving activity extends beyond the grave.

The second characteristic speaks powerfully to this last concern. It announces that God always acts in the best interest of the beloved. It must, accordingly, assert that God alone knows what is in the best interest of each of her children. Can it ever be in the best interest of a human soul to cast it into a blazing inferno forever? Of course not! Universalism maintains its strong position that God will lovingly act in the best interest of all his children, both in time and in eternity.

If this universalist view is not an accurate definition of agape love, then love must be redefined in such a way that it allows and oversees the unspeakable suffering of those "once loved" while on earth.

Why This Book

GIVEN THE NATURE OF the challenging, perhaps controversial, content of these writings, I will state the following reasons for sharing them now, and, as I hope, preserving them for consideration by future readers.

1. I am personally and totally committed to the proposition that the ultimate salvation of all is, in fact, the eternally correct interpretation of all things Christian, including the nature of God, the work of Jesus, and the mission of the church. I believe this, as I attempt to show, for philosophical, theological, and scriptural reasons.

2. It is my conviction that universal redemption offers immeasurable, much needed comfort and hope to all persons who have so often given someone into the hands of a mysterious, unwelcome, and dark death. They do so to this present day. They need no longer wonder about the eternal fate of their lost, dear ones.

3. Belief in universalism can unquestionably be a profound ingredient in the conduct of all human affairs at all levels—personal, interpersonal, national, and international. Its implications here are monumental.

4. I am decidedly grieved to hear anyone state: "I have lost my faith in Christianity." I affirm fearlessly and without apology that some interpretations of Christianity and some of its institutionalized forms ought well to be "lost"—given up or

PART ONE . . . in which I introduce the issues

discarded as ridiculous, faulty, illogical and simply wrong. Autobiographically, I can state that I have, indeed, "lost" or renounced many theological tenets and ideas. Over time, I came to see them as, in fact, anything but Christian.

I trust that it is not grandiose of me to wish and desire that many former believers would consider what is here, with the prospect that some of these ideas might better provide a solid foundation for theological reflection, for faith commitment, and for a possible new and intentional spiritual lifestyle. If the views in this book are accepted, one will have a decidedly new theology of God, Jesus, heaven and hell—therefore of Christianity.

5. I am equally concerned when someone states that he or she does not "believe in God." I profoundly respect that position, having known and seen scores of people live courageously, profoundly, even triumphantly in the face of their lack of belief in any Higher Power or any world to come.

However, when I encounter such a person, I am inclined to respond with an open-ended question like this: "Please tell me about the God you do not believe in. Perhaps I do not believe in that God either." While I have absolutely no intention to advance or endorse the faulty idea or notion of "proofs for the existence of God" (there are none), I do entertain the hope that even I, as a witness, may be able to present some information about the God I do believe in, and that my effort may be helpful.

Many people—not all—are exceedingly glad to hear that there is a God who is the God of eternal love for her creation and her creatures, and that this God has, truly, promised a blessed eternity for all. Such writings as these may offer welcome news for some who have, quite frankly, not heard of a God worthy of their belief!

6. I am grateful for the privilege of handing these pages to my friends in the fundamentalist-evangelical branches of the Christian faith. I am a "convert to Christ" as a result of God's

Spirit working through the ministry of many whose aim was to "save my soul." They toiled patiently and lovingly to keep me away from the infernal region of hell! I am eternally grateful.

I know their heart, their love, their zeal. I also know their fear. Sadly, many of them are severely conflicted, spiritually and psychologically, when they dare pause to think that the God who loves is the same God who eternally damns. They know that their strenuous efforts at "soul-saving" often fail, with the sad result of torment for those who do not properly respond.

I would wish for them some new convictions regarding their God, his son, and the final destiny of persons. Faith in the God who saves all should not dampen their spirits nor slacken their commitment to struggle for the good. It should, rather, offer them the joy, solace, and consolation of knowing that their desire for the salvation of people is precisely the desire and intention of the God they serve, and of the God who will assuredly accomplish it in eternity.

7. Finally, I write with the hope that future generations might "look it over." At my age, future generations means anyone younger, but I especially hope to gain an audience with those whom sociologists are labeling Generation Y and Generation Z. Research has identified their highly distinctive characteristics, traits, and habits. Others have spoken to the remarkable gifts of these youth, and those gifts are formidable.

My interest is in determining how predisposed they are to hear and accept anything much from their parents' "churches." They will clearly approach their spiritual investigation from entirely different perspectives than did their elders. After a career in parish ministry, my assessment is that they will find little that they are looking for. Is it likely, then, that they will seek association, identification, or much less "membership" in many of these established, Christian institutions? The existing denominations and their teaching will be deemed realities not able to command abiding, heartfelt

PART ONE . . . in which I introduce the issues

commitment. Why stay where needs are not met and implications for lifestyle cannot be genuinely and sincerely embraced? Generations Y and Z simply will not stay!

But here is my swelling optimism. I am certain that universalism has something to offer that is significant, profound, and compelling. Its ethic is love. Its goal is inclusion, not division. Its burden is to announce that God is desirous of eternal joy and bliss for everyone. Its "politics" is a muscular righteousness that attempts only the good. Its "economics" assures fairness and opportunity based upon individual human value. It proposes peace among all peoples and nations. It demands that we cherish and preserve our fragile planet and its non-human inhabitants. It stamps an eternal approval by God on the heart of every living creature.

I could go on and on. As its strong proponent, I see universal redemption as a most radical, revolutionary ideology, faith, and theology. It has yet to be given opportunity to exert its greatest impact and influence. Implementing and institutionalizing its tenets will rattle and shake foundations. So what?

My invitation is for all people to explore this theology and all its implications. I will watch with interest and excitement as they use their gifts and talents to take the eternal, all-embracing love of God into the sometimes unloved and unloving world. That message is very good news! Who will not welcome it?

Hell and God's Character

THE TITLE OF THIS book suggests an affirmation: God Will Save Us All. It suggests that the affirmation might be sustained and supported by Biblical teaching about the love of God. I believe it can.

As I say that, I acknowledge the fact that, happily, some parts of the Bible plainly teach this universal redemption. But I quickly admit that some of its pages teach just the opposite: God will not save us all.

If this is the case, and it is, how does one determine that God will or will not save the entirety of the human race? We are here, of course, interested only in "Bible teaching" on the subject.

People can be heard to state that if a teaching appears in the Bible once, it is pervasive teaching throughout. Hence, if there is one reference to eternal hell, then the doctrine is therefore forever taught and the entire Bible must be viewed through the lens of this teaching. This is not, however, one's best logical position. For why cannot the reverse be the case: if there is a clear reference to universal salvation, why cannot the entire Bible be viewed through the spectrum of that teaching?

I am sure that the various New Testament books separately endorse the doctrines of both eternal damnation and universalism. The better part of logical propriety is to simply accept the fact. I readily accept this obvious reality.

The task of the concerned thinker, then, will be to make a decision about which is "true," but of necessity based on other

25

PART ONE . . . in which I introduce the issues

grounds entirely. For honest interpreters, the text will not yield to one view over the other. Both are "right there!"

How then does one decide? In this book I declare that the criterion of greatest and highest value must be the character of Almighty God. I will ask which teaching is more in line with anything and everything we know and can learn about this God?

We can base our best understanding of that character on selected Old Testament passages, the authentic teachings of Jesus, the later Pauline theology, and on the message in several other New Testament books. The cumulative data is positively decisive for our purposes. I affirm eternal salvation for all because I affirm that it is perfectly in line with the revealed character of God.

Those advocating for an eternal torment have their texts. I rely on mine. Neither of us can "prove" anything conclusively or "beyond a shadow of a doubt." I will make my case as earnestly as I can. I honestly believe that on this topic, God's character is "on the line."

The Bible is a human book for humans to read and study. I think God's love is her dominant, eternally empowering attribute. It must lead to salvation for all. If God damns millions of souls to unrelenting suffering, her dominant characteristic can absolutely NOT be love. I think it will be POWER. That seems incontrovertible. If love can save but will not, that love is, by definition, far secondary to something else. I deny that it is! Perhaps better said, if love can save but love will not save, we must redefine love.

Who Is This God?

I HAVE ALREADY ANNOUNCED that God's attributes or characteristics are the foundation for any discussion of the ultimate fate of persons. It is God who created the universe and set in motion the entire process of cosmic history, inexorably leading to its God-intended conclusion. This world and every possible world, are in the ultimate control of this all-powerful diety. So, believers affirm.

It is quite appropriate for believers to inquire into the "motivation" of this God. After all, we are personally, and we presume eternally, involved in the playing-out of this mysterious drama. We might well desire to be better "acquainted" with the God who has created us, is now sustaining us, and who has very definite plans for the eternal destiny of her creation and creatures, including each one of us. How, indeed, is this God disposed toward us? What are the ways we can confidently find out? What can we say with a reasonable assurance that it is accurate?

These questions are not easy to answer. And we require a "source" for any knowledge we might come to possess. We seek absolute certainty, but we will have to live in a realm of ambiguity. Even so, there are ideas and concepts to which we can cling and in which we can hope.

It is certain that we cannot look to "nature" for answers. God's actions there, wondrous as they are, cannot help in determining what God "thinks" about human beings. While there is much to admire, marvel at, and be grateful for, the terrors of nature must also be factored in. For every beautiful mountain range, ocean

PART ONE . . . in which I introduce the issues

sunset, and healthy newborn baby, there are any number of catastrophic natural events which make our confidence shaky at best. We must look elsewhere than to nature to determine how God views us earthlings.

For those in the Judeo-Christian tradition, the Bible has been the only source for definitive data and accompanying belief. Here, too, the findings are not always satisfying. God is portrayed as a tribal tyrant, unconcerned about people and nations. She is quite willing to destroy and punish. He is wildly unfair, dealing unequally with individuals and large groups. All this and more can be found in the Bible rendering of who God is and how she acts. And regarding the subject of this work, it is easy to point to book, chapter, and verse wherein God is portrayed as unhesitatingly willing to cast untold millions into a fiery hell.

How have I, as author, made the decision to declare that God is complete love, and will save us all eventually? This entire book, and every essay, is given in an effort to answer that question. I have tried to make a plausible case for a confident faith in universalism. I am persuaded that it can be made, and I have given portions of my arguments in other essays. Here, I am inquiring into the attributes of God which seem pertinent to my concern.

Which attributes relate tellingly to considerations and questions about eternal hell? Let us explore these matters now. I have concluded that to properly address this issue, we need focus on three attributes only: love, wisdom, and power. I recognize that in God's "being," attributes and characteristics are not separable. The unity of God is the essence of God. However, we can and do converse about God's attributes separately.

I will formulate my questions thus: Is God powerful enough, wise enough, and loving enough to save all persons eternally? And if God does not save all eternally, what attribute must be dominant as the divine motivator?

I answer the first question with the most emphatic "Yes!" even as I ask a corollary question: Will God do it? Again, I answer with an obvious, "Yes."

Who Is This God?

Those believing in eternal torment must answer: If God can, but will not, save all persons, what will be the motivating reason? And much theological thought has gone into answering this, and to giving some sort of rationality for those reasons. Some of those reasons strain our cognitive abilities. Some are irrational and illogical. Most leave us with the definition of love which is shriveled and emaciated—unworthy of God!

Though I suspect that no believers in eternal torment would phrase it this way, this is the way it is: God is, of course, powerful enough to save all persons. God is, of course, wise enough to determine how to save all persons. But God is not loving enough to do it!

Why will God not? And the answers mount up rapidly: to do so, God would abandon her own "justice;" God will not countermand a human's "free will" decision to reject salvation; God will not violate the "clear teaching" of the Bible. And the list goes on.

The net effect of all these "reasons" is to effectively declare that they are more precious, dear, and important to God than are the creatures she has lovingly created. I do not think I am overstating or tastelessly exaggerating these eternally vital matters. Perhaps I am being too gentle here!

Let me declare that God's power is expressed in and by love, and that his wisdom is a function of love's purpose. And all other attributes and characteristics of our God find their meaning and definition as they are mediated through agape love. If this be not the case, everlasting suffering for millions, now and in the future, may be a shocking reality. But if love is supreme, there is no eternal torment awaiting anyone. Period.

The Book of 1 John declares that a summary of all that God is comes together in "love" (4:8). The Apostle Paul said that, "nothing shall separate us from the love of God" (Romans 8:38–39). Many believe that, on the contrary, several things can separate millions of persons from God's love, and that forever.

Paul was either right or wrong. Some teach that he was wrong. I think he was eternally right!

Because God Says So

IN THE LAST TWO hundred years, a cardinal principle of Christian theology has been slowly but surely relegated to the dustbin of history. It is the doctrine of divine decrees. There are understandable reasons for this, based on three strong objections, as I see it.

One is that the doctrine is the bedrock foundation for a very troubling notion of predestination. When one believes in eternal torment and that God has predetermined everything, from the foundation of the world, one is logically compelled to conclude that God has chosen some for salvation and the rest for damnation. There are many variations on this theology but the essential elements remain the same: the saved and the lost are known to God before they even exist; their eternal destinies are settled solely by God's choice, and this is without consideration of their deeds, merits, righteousness or lack thereof.

A second objection to the doctrine of decrees is that it makes human free will an irrelevant sham. Some theologians have even claimed that God and persons could not have free wills simultaneously!

Predictably, the philosophical reaction to this, in the Enlightenment and Post-Enlightenment, has gone to the other extreme, with persons now said to be endowed with absolute, even radical, free will. Some branches of Christianity teach that God does not decree salvation, but graciously offers it. Humans then accept or reject it by an action of the vaunted free will alone. This act secures salvation in heaven or eternal doom in hell. Everything turns on the human will.

A third objection to the older presentation of divine decrees is that it rightly raises questions about the moral character of God. When decrees are tied to an absolute predestination which denies the freedom of human will, what can one say about that God? The moral-ethical issue is correctly raised, for all definitions of right, wrong, love, mercy, justice, etc., are turned on their head, and become quite divorced from any ordinary human notions of the same words.

In this book, I am aggressively concerned to show that the character of God is the foundational issue here, and that that character is best understood and defined as agape love. Every attribute and action of God will, in God's time, be shown to be instrumental in achieving God's loving purposes and eternal outcomes for all.

These are three other thoughts.

One is that human free will is indeed a testy subject of inquiry. What are humans free to do or not free to do? How free are we, despite what we claim or would like to believe? This is not an essay about all that, but rather one to state this point: human free will is always contextual. As persons we are free in a certain context, which can be largely defined and which has definite parameters and limits. Some parts of my personal context I can do nothing about. Some parts of it I can expand or modify, opening new vistas for the further exercise of my freedom. This is obvious enough.

The relationship between these ideas and universal redemption is, of course, related and put in focus by asking: Is God powerful, wise, and loving enough to allow me free will, and also to obtain and secure my ultimate salvation? Can God bring me to heaven without taking away or violating my free will? And my answer is a categorical, "Yes!" The idea that this is such a momentous and contradictory position, and that God may not be able to "pull it off," is simply ludicrous!

We can catch a glimpse of what some such process might entail if we consider our human relationships, especially with children. Can wise, loving parents direct and encourage children to use their freedom in sensible, responsible ways? Of course. Do we negate their free wills as we attempt to expand or construct the environments in which they function? Not at all. From our vantage point, we can lovingly observe, assess, and provide the contexts which make for growth into mature personhood. Though sinners, we are, at least for a while, wiser and more knowledgeable than are they.

God is, of course, infinitely more knowledgeable, powerful, wise, and loving than his creatures—always. This is the fact that allows us as persons to function freely, but under the divine "direction" of this God of love.

My second point is this: if we disregard the idea of divine decrees, we have thrown out the proverbial "baby with the bath water." Here's why. Whatever is eternally true is eternally true because God says it is—or as I say, God decrees it. God does not discover truth; God speaks truth into being. The creation stories in Genesis declare that God said, "Let there be. . .," and it was so. These verses are perfect examples of divine decrees. The scriptures are replete with such affirmations.

God is not waiting around in heaven to see what he will do with the souls of his children. She has already decreed the eternal outcome. God will save us all because she says she will save us all. This is a divine decree, and like dozens of others, is irrevocable. (The topic of what God freely chooses to know or not to know is beyond the scope of this essay and book.)

The Apostle Paul uses the very word in Romans 11 (to be discussed below). Verse 26—God will save all Israel. Verse 29—God's call is irrevocable. Verse 32—God will have mercy on all. God does predestine, after all. But it is a predestination which maintains human free will, with the ultimate outcome foreseen before the worlds began: God will save everyone he has ever created, for the Lord God has spoken it!

My final thought on the decrees centers on the relationship between the decrees and the person and work of Jesus. In the first centuries of its existence, the church endured several highly contentious ecumenical councils. These early gatherings helped establish much of its doctrine and teaching.

A challenging goal, revisited in many councils, was to achieve agreement on definitive language for defining Christology, as the doctrine is called. While the "fathers" finally came to a concensus formula on the person of Jesus, they were never able to satisfactorily describe what Jesus had effectively done for the salvation of persons. This area of theology is called "soteriology," from a combination of Greek words. The focus is on human redemption, salvation, being "born again," being "saved," and similar, familiar notions. And the church has not, to this very day, adequately described or defined how the life and death of Jesus actually "saves" anyone.

If universal salvation is a reality due to the predeterminate counsel and decree of God, before the foundation of the world, the role of Jesus may be part and parcel of that decree. His role would then be instrumental, not determinative. What is it, in this scenario, that the earthly Jesus contributes to the plan for ultimate, universal human redemption?

To assert that the work of Jesus is the essential component of the initial decree merely moves the equation back one step. We are no closer to identifying the salvific mechanism and process. Even turning directly to the New Testament brings us no closer to an answer. To say that Jesus' life, death, even his resurrection "saves," as many verses teach, is a declarative statement. It does not tell us "how."

We suspect that we are asking a richly meaningful, if unanswerable question. Even if the mystery is beyond imponderable, we are left with the inescapable fact that New Testament Christians believed that Jesus was their "savior." Something had happened to them, individually and collectively, to produce this heartfelt response to his life and teaching. And throughout history millions more have made the same confession. Something occurs which identifies Jesus with one's experience of renewal and rebirth. It is considered profoundly real and life changing.

PART ONE . . . in which I introduce the issues

Since the beginning of human history, several billions of persons have lived and died without any awareness or knowledge of the life of Jesus of Nazareth. If that life is somehow determinative of the ultimate salvation of them all, such a revelation can be manifested only in the ages to come, and that only by God herself.

The Apostle Paul stated his belief that "at the name of Jesus every knee should bow, of things in heaven, in earth, and under the earth" (Phil. 2:10). Even if he believed that all of human salvation will culminate in an acknowledgement of the unique role of Jesus, even Paul knew that such an event would occur only after an indefinite amount of kairos, which is God's time.

God Is Responsible

CHRISTIANITY IS FULL OF mysteries. Mysteries meaning that human beings can ask questions that human beings cannot answer. Ostensibly, only God can. (Unless the question is linguistic nonsense!)

One such burning question is this: why is God so permissive of sin and evil? The question does not apply only to human creatures. It applies to human tragedy and suffering, of course, but also to animal pain and to the degrading of nature and the environment.

Thousands of pages have been written by the brightest minds in history, but in the end the question is ever before us in bold relief. We have no choice but to be "satisfied" intellectually and spiritually with the only answer available: if one believes in God, this matter is God's affair, and in God's good time there will be resolution and completion. Satisfactory, it is not. Our real and pressing problem is that we encounter the question daily as we live our lives, and that sin and suffering are as real as any component part of our existence.

We cannot, however, "demand an answer" from God, with facts and figures to satisfy our deepest yearnings, outrage, or strong curiosity. Even if it is human nature to ask, every aspect of human nature does not command God's notice or response. We suspect, then, that our rightful task must be to fight and struggle, as best we can, against every manifestation of sin and evil, confident that

PART ONE . . . in which I introduce the issues

God will reveal whatever God chooses to reveal, in God's eternal time, kairos.

In actuality, we survive each day in this "world of woe," and much of the time life is wonderful beyond our expectations and deserts. God does sustain us now, and that is prospective of her sustaining us eternally. The term for what we are to be exhibiting "here below" is trust. We trust that God will orchestrate a holy outcome of blessing and grace. The mystery is unsettling and real, but we forge ahead in faith, sustained by what we can understand. Despair is not an option because of what we believe about the outcome.

One sustaining grace in all of this is the truth taught by universalism: all evil and sin must be destroyed forever. God will overcome every resistance, power, and dominion in accomplishing this feat. It is, in fact, the goal of love's saving activity in both time and eternity.

This, however, can never be a reality if a hell of unending torment actually exists. If it does, then this is the mind-jolting fact: there will be a place where unrepented and unforgiven sin, committed by unforgiven sinners, exists for all eternity! God's only activity vis-à-vis this hell is to inflict pain and suffering (or "allow" it) on these hapless souls, and that forever and ever.

And let there be no mistake about the shocking implication from this: the identity of the one responsible for the pain can only be God. Indeed, the ultimate responsibility for whatever happens in hell or heaven lies with the creator and sustainer of them both. There is no "passing the buck" to others. God will be doing it actively, not passively. That logic is unassailable.

The mystery of God's permissiveness of sin and evil is "solved" in one of two ways. God will comfortably oversee a place of true hellishness filled with human misery, suffering, sin, and evil—with God actively permitting it—forever. Or, God will eventually destroy all evil and oversee a heavenly realm populated by redeemed, purified, and reconciled souls, and that forevermore.

As human creatures we simply cannot fathom the reasons why God has chosen to create and order the world this way.

Nothing in our cognitive repertoire will quite satisfy our deep yearning to know. But we cannot know. We await revelations from God appropriate to our eternally evolving abilities to grasp what God chooses to commit to those she is saving.

The mystery of God's permissiveness is God's "problem," not ours. God does require us, however, to engage with him in the struggle to overcome sin and evil in our lives and in the lives of others. That will also be God's eternal work in our lives, as we will see in essays to come. Now, we partner with God in redeeming the world! If we do not, we are adding to the sin and evil that must be destroyed. We have that choice!

PART TWO

...in which I turn to the Bible

Inspired, Inerrant, Infallible?

ONE OF THE MOST self-serving assertions in the history of scholarship may be this: the original autographs of all 66 books in the Bible were verbally inspired by God and were, therefore, in those originals, inerrant and infallible. The entire edifice of Biblical fundamentalism is built on this interesting claim. There are, however, some serious problems for this position.

1. There is no historical or archaeological evidence for the existence of such autographs.
2. No Bible writer ever claims knowledge of such autographs.
3. No Bible writer makes such a claim for the material he is writing.
4. The disappearance of these autographs is quite mysterious since they would have been considered the holiest writing in Judeo-Christian literature, and been preserved at all costs. Yet, all 66 are gone!
5. Within a few years of their supposed composition, in the New Testament era at least, the synoptic gospels appeared, demonstrating considerable differences and variations in detailing the life and teachings of Jesus. Had there been definitive texts, this occurrence would appear highly unlikely and a clear example of unfaithfulness to those originals. Surely some member of the faith community would have read the originals and then noted the significant changes in the later documents.

PART TWO ... in which I turn to the Bible

6. Is it conceivable that God would verbally inspire the most important literature in the history of the world only to abandon it to total oblivion within a very short span of time?

7. No human writer would assuredly know that he had penned a God-breathed manuscript.

8. No human writer could present irrefutable evidence to others that he had produced inspired literature.

9. Even if an ancient or a modern scribe had possession of the 66 original autographs, she or he could not demonstrate convincingly that they were inspired, inerrant, or infallible.

10. No modern fundamentalist can offer irrefutable evidence demonstrating that any book in the Bible is derived from an earlier original inspired autograph.

11. Fundamentalism's claims about the text are simply a witness to a set of beliefs, not "proof" of the correctness of those beliefs.

12. Fundamentalism exists because a group of human believers agree to view the Bible a certain way.

13. Fundamentalism's position must logically be that standards established outside the Bible are said to be found in the Bible or are to be applied to the Bible.

14. None of these standards can be convincingly defined or demonstrated under any circumstances.

Nevertheless, many readers of my essays sincerely believe that these familiar terms undeniably apply to the Bible: inspired, inerrant, and infallible. Believing that, they will have strong objections to my approach to the scriptures. This is not the place to engage those three terms in close definition or further theological scrutiny. I will simply ask what I already alluded to: where did the criteria for determining this inspiration, inerrancy, and infallibility originate? There is only one answer. They must, by default, arise outside the text to which they are applied.

Inspired, Inerrant, Infallible?

They are, therefore, of human origin entirely. Insofar as that is so, one must face the awkward reality, to many, that something outside the Bible is determining the status of the Bible. And this line of reasoning can go on indefinitely: Where do the extra-Biblical standards come from? Are they inspired, inerrant, and infallible? Who says so?

It will not quite do to state this: "the Bible is inspired, inerrant, and infallible because the Bible says it is." Prominent people actually hold this circular position. It is an example of the fallacy of self-authentification: something is true because it claims to be true. If this criterion is held to be valid, then how many other sacred books, texts, and scriptures will be allowed the same standard of legitimacy? Many Christians shudder to think that the texts of other religions may be granted the same status as the Bible. That would completely undermine their essential theology and teaching.

We have no evidence that any writer(s) of any New Testament book ever affirmed or implied that their finished work was inspired, inerrant, or infallible. Whoever made those claims lived years or centuries later. It appears then that no rigid system of Biblical interpretation should be built upon the conclusions that unknown persons asserted centuries ago under equally unknown circumstances.

Here is a very significant point, so obvious as to seem embarrassingly unnecessary to even state: there is no verse in the Bible about the Bible. There are plenty of references to utterances, words, and visions that are equated with holy writ or with the "word of God." But none of these can be said to refer to our Bible. Any interpretation, of any verse, which concludes that is a reference to the compilation of books now known as the Bible, is simply incompetent scriptural interpretation.

However, did Jesus not say, "My words will not pass away?" (Mt. 24:35; Mk. 13:31). These are precious verses to all the faithful, to be sure. But, they have been made into something even Jesus had not intended. Was he referring to the Bible? Of course, not. Do we have all his words? No. Then, did some "pass away?" Yes.

PART TWO . . . in which I turn to the Bible

All the gospels declare that Jesus did and said many things that are not recorded. What happened to them? They passed into history, never to be retrieved.

And, yes, the writer of 2 Timothy said plainly: "All Scripture is inspired by God" (3:16). But he had said in 3:15 that Timothy had known the holy Scriptures since infancy! Is 3:15 a reference to the Bible? Of course not. It refers to the ancient Scriptures of Israel. Neither the New Testament, nor 2 Timothy itself, for that matter, is being discussed.

The Bible was written by those who knew God and were known by God. That was all the "inspiration" they needed to pen their books. There are many theories about that inspiration, but in the end the situation has never changed. The church acknowledges 66 books in its Bible, 39 in the Old Testament and 27 in the New. All Christian comment revolves around discussion of the contents of those recognized books. It will forever be so.

The Bible is certainly God's providential gift to the church, and the church, by consensus, continues to affirm its primacy in faith matters (even as it passionately debates many of those matters). The church existed hundreds of years before the Bible was compiled and organized. The interplay and interaction between church and Bible is a large part of the story of ecclesiastical history. We are certain that the "rediscovery" of the Bible in the 16th century led to the Protestant Reformation, as church leaders grappled with new definitions of such Biblical terms as "faith" and "justification by faith," among others.

In 1620, during that Reformation, before the nonconformist Congregationalists left Leiden, Holland, on board the good ship, Speedwell, Pastor John Robinson preached a sermon to those "Pilgrims." In it, he said, "For I am very confident that the Lord hath more truth and light yet to break forth out of his Holy Word." Perhaps his congregants thought he simply meant that the more one studies the Bible, the more one will learn about it, and that the learning will be fathomless. Even as I am no scholar, I would agree.

But perhaps he meant that in unknowable ways the Bible can break forth in brilliant new light, as new ideas about God and the faith flash into view. Pastor Robinson died before he saw the New World with his congregation. But surely he was right. We can all yet see a new world in Biblical studies as each generation attends to that word and discovers its richness anew.

The beautiful Collect for the Second Sunday in Advent, from the 1928 Book of Common Prayer, requires no inspired, inerrant, and infallible document. It simply acknowledges and celebrates the most wondrous gift of the Bible.

"Blessed Lord, who has caused all holy Scriptures to be written for our learning: Grant that we may in such wise hear them, read, mark, learn, and inwardly digest them, that by patience, and comfort of thy holy Word, we may embrace, and ever hold fast the blessed hope of everlasting life, which thou hast given us in our Savior Jesus Christ. Amen."

We Cannot Do "Biblical Theology"

I HAVE STATED THAT this book is based upon Biblical theology and Biblical interpretation. All of the six premises on which it is based make direct or indirect reference to holy scripture, as I understand it. Anyone who believes in unending torment will predictably object to all six of my premises, denying that they reflect any proper or correct Biblical interpretation or theology. I will direct some comments to that point.

I believe it is quite impossible, in our current age, for one to do "Biblical theology" as the term has historically been used in most Christian circles. By that I mean that for hundreds of years theologians and scholars tried to view the Bible as a "whole." They attempted to blend and shuffle scripture with the idea in mind to present "what the Bible teaches." That process was always doomed to disastrous failure, especially among those who could be called, by their own choice, fundamentalists. The Bible teaches many things, some quite contradictory.

Our scripture contains 66 books, 39 in the Old Testament, 27 in the New. Often interpreters have refused to understand that the two testaments cannot be conflated. They stand alone for interpretive usages. The Apostle Paul reminds us that the Old Testament brings us to Jesus the Christ, that it is read for its examples, that it is a tutor, that it is not "law" for Christians, that, in his words, it was "nailed to the cross." All of this from a true scholar whose life work had been to study, interpret, and to teach those same Jewish scriptures.

We Cannot Do "Biblical Theology"

Unless interested in historical or Jewish studies, Christians must read the Old Testament through the lens of the New. Whatever ethical or moral teaching is not carried over from the Old into the New is not binding on followers of Jesus. A perfect example of this kind of transition occurs in viewing the Ten Commandments. Nine of the ten are repeated as teachings to be observed by Christians. One is not. "Remember the Sabbath to keep it holy" can be turned into "Remember the first day of the week..." only by sleight of hand. The Christian command to worship on Sunday is taught by indirect command or example, unless Hebrews 10:25 refers to "going to church." Dozens of similar examples could be cited, making my point.

Having stated that "Biblical theology" cannot be written with both testaments in mind, I ask: can one write a "Theology of the New Testament," my main scriptural concern. I maintain that it cannot be done. My reasoning begins with the fact that modern scholarship precludes it. The 27 books are not a linked chain of thought or of theology. In this book, I acknowledge the major differences in teachings between the four gospels. The remaining 23 books present the same reality of significant divergences. They agree on many things, while pointedly disagreeing on others.

I need to state that I was initially trained as a fundamentalist. That is a mindset which dictates that the entire Bible be assessed as "God-inspired" and "God-given." The corollary from such a view is, obviously, that the Bible must indeed by interpreted as a "whole," and that it is a seamless web. Since God oversaw its entire composition and preservation, it must be "all of a kind." God cannot contradict God!

I can give personal examples of the implications from such a position. I once believed that in order "to be saved," everyone had to profess faith in Jesus Christ in this life. I believed that baptism by immersion was essential for that salvation, and that it was taught by the entire New Testament. And, in line with the subject of this book, I of course believed that an unending hell awaited unrepentant sinners, and that all the New Testament endorsed that concept. I was looking at the 27 books as a compact unit, and in

PART TWO . . . in which I turn to the Bible

so doing superimposed the theological presuppositions of fundamentalism on the whole text. I was wrong!

Of the six premises on which I have written these essays, all deal with Biblical interpretation. I affirm that the character of God is best determined by a careful review of selected texts in both the Old and New Testaments, and definitively in the life and words of Jesus. I affirm that Jesus did not teach unending hell. I use the methods of higher and lower criticism to reinforce my belief. I state that Paul believed in eternal hell, and wrote that he did. In some way, undisclosed to us, he changed his mind, then wrote repeatedly about his new thinking. We have direct access to those writings. I believe some of the remaining New Testament books teach universal redemption, and clearly some do not. These books are available for our discerning study and reflective review. Even my speculations about the nature of hell and the afterlife are Biblically grounded by verses that demand expanded thought and consideration. They literally tease us into serious deliberation.

My essays here are limited to the doctrine of life in an age to come only. If all the multiple doctrines of the Christian faith are overlaid the books of the New Testament, no scholar or student should affirm a unified and unbroken theology of any doctrine. It is a fruitless undertaking and quite simply needless. I am reiterating that "Biblical Theology" cannot be done. Neither can "Old Testament" or "New Testament Theology."

So, what is left? We can, in New Testament studies, legitimately do only the theology of a particular book, or "school" of books. One can do the theology of the Matthean school, the Johannine school, Mark, Jude, the early Paul, the late Paul, and on through the contents of the New Testament (as well as the Old.) After that, one can do comparative analyses of the findings, if that is a goal.

Naturally, some similar teachings occur in more than one book. They are, after all, witnesses to the life and work of Jesus. On the other hand, no book is a mirror image of any other. They were written for different reasons, to different audiences, from different points of view. All that in separate times and from different

We Cannot Do "Biblical Theology"

places. They have independent status, and must be so viewed by anyone responsibly approaching the text. Every other interpretive enterprise is forced, artificial, and a "reading into" the text, rather than "leading out" of the text its proper meaning. In New Testament Greek terms, this is the crucial difference between eisegesis and exegesis.

Eisegesis superimposes an interpretive teaching or point of view onto the text. Exegesis leads out of the text its intended teaching. As an approach to Biblical interpretation, fundamentalism is largely eisegesis.

Fundamentalism's tacit message is this: when approaching a text of scripture, the reader must first remember that it is inspired, infallible, and inerrant. I maintain that this thinking superimposes on the text an unnecessary and unwarranted limitation and constraint, and that such an approach may seriously hinder an adequate understanding of the message and meaning of the text. I say again that fundamentalism is pure eisegesis.

The Johannine redactor left us a provocative text in Revelation 22:18-19: "Woe to anyone who adds to or takes away from the words of this book." He means, of course, his own writing. I say, "Woe to anyone who declares that certain things are in the Bible as a whole, which are not, and woe to everyone who will not say what is in the separate books of the Bible, regardless of whether one agrees with it or happens not to like it." Let the Bible be the Bible, not a text descended directly from heaven by any God. We may call it divine only if we acknowledge that it has been mediated through the minds and hands of real live people who believed in and served God.

How To Write A Gospel

THE THEOLOGICAL AND COSMIC implications from the life and teaching of Jesus are found in 23 New Testament books, while the "story" of his deeds and words is found in only the four gospels.

Church leaders agreed upon the contents of our "canon," the Bible, hundreds of years after Jesus' death. There has been ongoing debate, for centuries, about which books should be in or out of that canon. When it comes to study of the gospels, related questions and problems abound on every hand.

A concern arises immediately when it is discovered that the gospels themselves were not documents contemporaneous with Jesus, but were written years or decades after he lived and died. Additionally, we have no evidence that Jesus actually committed anything to writing. Furthermore, there is nothing to indicate that the gospel writers have merely recorded verbatim a contemporary utterance of Jesus. We can go on: there is no indication whatever that a writer is simply translating a statement of Jesus from his native language, Aramaic, into the language of the gospel composition, Greek. And, of course, no disciple followed Jesus "taking notes" of his words and actions for recording later on. Finally this: though many Christian teachers and students are unconcerned about it, Biblical scholars to this day continue to discuss the authorship, composition, order, and proper wording for numerous verses in the gospels.

Given all this verified and factual data, where did all the material come from that has ended up written down in our gospels? The

How To Write A Gospel

earliest church, then, had no "New Testament." When members preached, taught, worshipped, or evangelized they had use only of oral traditions, written fragments, and narratives of Jesus' words and deeds. Naturally, different communities possessed different source materials, and valued and cherished them as sacrosanct.

When it was decided to create a gospel, collating, comparing, arranging, deleting, correcting, and editorializing were all activities and functions of editors, scribes, and redactors. The shrouds of history have fallen over the next acts in this fascinating process, but our intuition is most certainly correct: the gospels were created by concerned followers of Jesus to be presented to certain identifiable audiences for very specific reasons. Some of that reasoning and intentionality is forever lost to us. Some is not, and can be demonstrated. In any event, by the year 100 C.E., Matthew, Mark, Luke, and John were documents available to the world, and destined to change it, by any accounting.

The concern of this book is to announce that God will save us all in God's good time. A sub-theme must be an affirmation that Jesus of Nazareth did not believe in, nor teach, unending hell. He was confident that his heavenly Parent was, even in his own lifetime, actively engaged in that universal redemption, and that he, Jesus, was a witness to, and a unique part, of its accomplishment. How does this current essay and study of gospel composition relate to legitimizing these claims about Jesus. I will address that now.

We can begin our spadework with an almost self-evident premise: any follower of Jesus, attempting to record his life and teaching, would do nothing intentional to falsify or skew that record. One could not be a disciple of this man if one set out to misrepresent him or to mislead readers about him. However, the writers did not approach their task completely devoid of theological presuppositions. Their ultimate belief was, of course, that Jesus was eternally and cosmically significant. They held any number of other ideas and theological beliefs, as well.

What if a gospel writer read or heard a saying of Jesus and thought its meaning incomplete, or that it needed further elaboration? What if this disciple-writer was totally confident that he

PART TWO . . . in which I turn to the Bible

knew categorically what Jesus "really meant" to say? And what if such a writer-editor redactor simply put those words in the mouth of Jesus? It is quite understandable to think it possible. It is rather more than possible, for it happened repeatedly.

Credulity cannot be stretched far enough to believe that the collected fragments and narratives in the writer's materials contained such detail as: "On this day, at this time, in this place, Jesus was standing with disciple A and B, and as he gazed out over the hills or sea or temple, he said. . ." Understanding this, one can readily assess what a gospel writer had to "add" to a deed-saying in order to place it in his own narrative history.

Today, we can use the word "contextualize" to describe this writing situation. Certainly sayings-deeds did not come with a complete social—historical context. The gospel writers and editors, therefore, created those contexts. This is precisely why many of the sayings of Jesus, with almost the exact wording, appear in different times and places in the synoptics. The writer had access to the saying. He then had to develop a place and time and circumstance in which to locate the saying. The same is true in the handling of Jesus' many deeds. It is no more complicated than that.

The alternative to this deliberate approach was, of course, to simply compile a list of Jesus' deeds and words and to write them down in some order of the editor's own choosing. A non-biblical "gospel," the Gospel of Thomas, does just that. The book is a long series of the sayings of Jesus.

Our gospel editors were far more creative: they gave to the ages the new genre of "gospel," a theological historical narrative of the life, sayings, and deeds of the completely unique one, Jesus of Nazareth.

A final consideration here is this: given their presuppositions and theological beliefs that Jesus held views in line with theirs, what would the gospel writers want conveyed about Jesus' beliefs? What did they want us to believe that he believed? Could their presentation of Jesus be radically different from what Jesus actually believed and taught? With reference to his belief in and teachings about eternal torment for untold millions, I am quite sure of it!

Just A Little Help

WE CAN UNDERSTAND SCRIPTURE better if we keep in mind a few simple things as we read. Students of the New Testament will often encounter the word "synoptic." The term is derived from the Greek words for "view" and "together." For most of Christian history readers have recognized that Matthew, Mark, and Luke can be viewed together "synoptically." That is, they have many, many similarities and commonalities. Likewise, it has been noted that the Gospel of John cannot be so viewed, since its completed form is decidedly unlike the synoptics.

We have stated above that redactors, scribes, and editors collected the sayings-deeds material about Jesus and put them into a narrative that resulted in the individual gospel accounts.

It is easy to demonstrate aspects of this editing process. One can literally lay similar passages from the synoptics side by side. The wording can be seen to match very closely or to deviate noticeably. These variances can be detected in story-event-deed-saying that is unquestionably the same, single event in Jesus' life. This method of study can be facilitated by use of a readily available text with the synoptics in columns, called gospel parallels. The relationship between the writers and editors of our gospels is an ongoing scholarly enterprise, not to concern us here, however.

Historically, the church has been irresponsibly remiss in not studying these scriptures in a truly synoptic fashion. It has been almost dismissive of the substantial variations in the accounts of the same events. The church should be quite willing to acknowledge

PART TWO . . . in which I turn to the Bible

these obvious discrepancies and ask, "Why did they occur?" There are several good reasons, and some of them are theologically potent, as we shall see.

If the idea of synoptic study of the gospels is valued, readers of the New Testament also realize another important characteristic of the text: it contains both literal and figurative language. That is true of books in both the Old Testament and the New. It is also true of the recorded words of Jesus.

There are any number of types of figurative language, and many were employed by Jesus. He spoke using simile, metaphor, hyperbole, proverb, parable, joke-pun, paradox, and irony. He asked questions routinely. He utilized poetry from the Old Testament. He also used several other less familiar figures of speech: metonymy, personification, and synecdoche.

We can cite example after example of Jesus' use of non-literal terms. Here are four. He called Peter a "rock" as well as "Satan." He is recorded referring to James and John as "Sons of Thunder." He stated that he would have gathered children as a "hen gathers her brood." He said that "the stones might shout out," in praise to God.

We do not think Jesus was confused or that he mistook the solid, sometimes stubborn Peter for the Evil One. He referred to James and John as "Sons of Thunder," not because they were descended from stormy clouds, but because of their dispositions, we assume. He stated that he would have gathered children as a mother hen, not because he was unsure about this poultry self-reference, but because he felt the care and concern of a protecting parent. He said stones might shout, not because he thought they would, but because all nature ascribes praise in its time.

Since it is obviously the case that Jesus relied heavily on these commonplace forms of communication, students should ask how that fact applies as we address the sayings about eternal torment.

Jesus would have been well aware that his audience of Pharisees and "common people" believed that Gehenna-hell was, indeed, a real place of timeless, fiery suffering. However, his use of the term would not thereby mean that he subscribed to those definitions, or that he was being dishonest or disingenuous in

Just A Little Help

intentionally using the term. He could have used it in a wholly figurative sense, for many different reasons.

In only eight sayings in the gospels, is it recorded that Jesus used the Greek term, Gehenna, usually translated, hell. Does he mean that dreadful place of non-stop suffering each time he has used it? No, he does not, as we shall see below.

The use of figurative language is a very common practice among all linguistic peoples, and examples in our own time are easily forthcoming. Jesus used such language regularly in his daily discourse.

If students need to be aware of the concept of comparing gospel writings, and of types of language used in discourse by Jesus, there is another important observation to be made here. It relates to Jesus' recorded actions, and not to his words.

We must look carefully at these acts in terms of their symbolism. What does Jesus mean to teach or convey, not so much by what he says as by what he does?

My opinion is that from the first days of his active ministry until his death on a cross, Jesus' behaviors are multilayered in intentional meaning. This fact has long been recognized and is a fruitful study. Its pertinence here relates to my assertion that Jesus did not teach unending hell and torment. I am saying that both his words and actions can be analyzed for their figurative symbolism. Examples are too numerous to consider, but a couple make my point that Jesus' actions point toward the establishment of the realm of God, in which all-inclusive love is the central feature.

At the beginning of his ministry, Jesus is baptized by John. Why? John's baptism was for the "forgiveness of sins." Matthew's writers have Jesus state that John should baptize him "to fulfill all righteousness." That, of course, explains nothing. I believe Jesus submits to John in order to identify with an emergent new Israel, which is now declaring its willingness to repent and obediently participate in the coming new kingdom of God.

Jesus chooses twelve disciples. Why not more or less? This is clear enough if one remembers that Jesus is calling attention to the Twelve Tribes of Israel, and that they were God's people chosen

PART TWO . . . in which I turn to the Bible

to bring light to all nations. They failed. This newly elected Israel must complete that ministry, under Jesus' lead and tutelage.

Jesus eats with tax collectors and prostitutes. The religious leaders of his day were mortified by such scandalous behavior. Why do it? Is Jesus modeling what we should do, regardless of our reputation or the chance for fleshly temptation? I think, rather, he is proclaiming that as the true son, his Parent—God desires to claim and to include all people in the realm of his sovereignty, regardless of where they are initially in spiritual growth and maturity. They, too, belong to God.

Jesus cleanses the temple in a very aggressive, even militaristic way. Why? Is this the gentle "lamb of God," the "come unto me" Jesus? Is this a program for us to imitate when we confront hypocrisy and greedy commerce infiltrating the institutions of God? I suspect it is a cleansing (not understood in John's gospel) that boldly shouts to the religious leaders to prepare the holy places for an inauguration in power of the presence of the living God.

This illustrating of Jesus' symbolic behaviors and actions, to demonstrate my point, could be extended profitably. I will stop here.

If many of Jesus' actions must be viewed symbolically, the same claim seems applicable to many of his words, including some pertaining to the fires of an unending hell. I will attempt to elucidate this further in other essays.

Saying "Hell" In The Gospels

Though other "gospels" circulated in early church history, Christians have ended up with the four in our Bibles. I will make some general comments about the synoptic gospels, followed by comments, in the next essay, about the Gospel of John.

Many scholars believe that Mark was written by the disciple Mark, of New Testament fame. Luke, as well, was written by the New Testament personage, Luke. He wrote the Book of Acts in addition. Luke-Acts was supposedly one book or manuscript in original composition, but they are now separated by the Gospel of John in our New Testaments. Authorship issues are not particularly important, except when there are glaring examples of theological significance. That is true for the topic of these essays, eternal hell.

There is general scholarly agreement that the Gospel of Matthew was not written by a disciple named Matthew. The book was the product of a "school," a term used to describe a group of scribes, redactors, and editors working to produce the finished text. These men—we assume they all were—pored over the sayings-deeds collections and accounts and shaped them into the Gospel we have today.

Matthew scholars point to Syria as the likely place of its composition. Syria was miles from Jerusalem—Galilee, Jesus' familiar surroundings, and the area in which Jesus' influence would have remained more pronounced. Many of the sayings-deeds that ended up in Matthew's school must obviously reflect the corporate thinking of the Syrian Christians. Many of those Christians were

PART TWO ... in which I turn to the Bible

converts from Judaism, steeped in the teachings of the Pharisees. It is well known that the Pharisees did, and the school of Matthew did, accordingly, believe in the doctrine of unending hell. This is a highly significant point in answering the question, "Did Jesus Teach Eternal Torment?"

That Matthew's scribes endorsed this view with strong intensity and zealous emphasis can be demonstrated by a simple exercise: we will now identify, in each synoptic Gospel, all the supposed utterances of Jesus dealing with Gehenna, hell, torment, and unending doom. This is a relatively easy task. Many have done it, and the results of this analysis yield startling data. There is one such passage in Mark. There is one such passage in Luke. However, there are ten such passages in Matthew. In the synoptics, there are only eight sayings, recorded as spoken by Jesus, using the Greek word, Gehenna, for hell.

Perhaps this proves nothing about Jesus' teaching. Perhaps it shows that the doctrine of hell was not a paramount focus of the writers and audiences of Mark and Luke. But perhaps it reinforces the surface conclusion that, without question, the school of Matthew had a peculiar, telling interest in the end times, and the doctrine of unending torment. Then might we wonder if, perhaps, this fact says more about the teaching of Matthew's scribal editors than it does about the teaching of Jesus. I think so.

The ratio of Matthew 10, Luke 1, and Mark 1, is fraught with implications for interpreters. If one of Jesus' primary missions was to save souls from hellish doom, as many affirm, we might think that Luke and Mark would have many more verses on the subject. They do not. Given these facts, I am convinced, therefore, that we have linguistic, spiritual and theological permission to rethink the issues as we ask: Did Matthew's writers believe in eternal torment? Certainly. Did Mark and Luke? Very likely. Did Jesus of Nazareth?

Jesus was certainly not a theologian as the term is now defined. It is clearly apparent that in his life he never preached a plain and simple sermon on "universal redemption" per se (or on any other "theological topic," for that matter.) None is recorded. It is also demonstrably true that in the four gospels he never says that any person is going to eternal hell, nor that anyone is there now. Surely, had the latter concern been foremost in his mind, he would have been beyond forceful in his preaching and teaching. After all, he was the one about whom the issue was now raised. He, himself, was the one to be accepted or rejected, believed in or not, with the direst of eternal consequences in play. But not a word about accepting his lordship or unending, fiery doom. No one who believes in eternal, punishing hell can give a convincing explanation for this striking fact and monumental oversight.

Despite this undeniable truth, the history of Christian thinking and proclamation has proceeded as if all that Jesus talked about was saving souls from hell. It would seem to imply that on every page of the four gospels Jesus was urging and encouraging a proper audience response and action to avoid the hellish ramparts. One looks in vain for such scriptural passages. They do not exist.

What does exist are numerous sayings and deeds whereby Jesus is demonstrating or transparently stating the open, accepting, inviting eternal love of his Father-Mother God, and that for all manner of women and men. Jesus is as perfectly clear about this all-inclusive, all-embracing love, as he is deadly silent about the prospect of a literal, agonizing hell for any of God's dear children, including those who would reject him as their "personal savior." Multitudes did reject him. What did he say to God about all the tongue-wagging, finger-pointing scoffers at the foot of the cross? Is there one word about the assured prospect that they are all going to an unending, hellish torment? No, there is not. Rather, "Father, forgive them."

John's Gospel
Based On A True Story

The Gospel of John will not be considered in my study of Jesus' teaching on torment and hell. There are several reasons for the decision.

This gospel simply cannot be viewed synoptically with the other gospels. Its life of Jesus unquestionably cannot be harmonized with his life, deeds, and sayings as presented in the synoptics. It is almost as if two different "theological lives" are being described. Perhaps they are.

In our time we often see motion pictures "based on a true story." That is a perfect descriptor for the gospel of John—a creative, brilliant, often stunningly beautiful interpretation of the life of Jesus. There may be authentic sayings-deeds, and true teachings of Jesus in the book, but they are nearly impossible to extract from the finely-woven interpretive narrative. Even where John does not contradict the synoptics, the material must be read with extreme caution. The "historical Jesus" is difficult enough to discern in the synoptics, nearly impossible in John's highly stylized account.

A "School of John," not the New Testament disciple, produced this gospel, and also the books of 1, 2, 3 John, and the book of Revelation. Johannine scholars discern some common threads in these five books, leading to the one school conclusion. The composition, order, and theology of John's gospel is a technical and fascinating study for interested students. Those studies need not detain us, except for a few comments.

John's Gospel

The content of John's source material has led his editors to some major additions and omissions as we compare it with the synoptics. There are many. A few examples and comments follow. Who, indeed, remembered, then recorded for this gospel, the numerous, lengthy, expansive prayers, teachings and pronouncements of Jesus when he was said to be alone or nowhere near a secretary or scribe? This large and rich accumulation of material is unlike any in the synoptics. Were these narrative productions creative artistry at its best (as I maintain), or do these long, wordy sayings contain vestiges of Jesus' authentic utterances that we can never successfully recapture? We ask in vain about this wondrous material.

The Gospel of John mysteriously contains no parables. Though highly touted by Jesus in the synoptics as an indispensable teaching method, John has no such stories. This is yet another instance of the almost completely independent authorship of John, leaving more darkness than light on the questions regarding composition.

John's writers have found unpersuasive, if known to them, the gospel of Mark's need to maintain the so called "Messianic secret," wherein Jesus forbids demons and disciples from making his true identity known. John, on the other hand, has Jesus and others robustly acknowledge or declare openly that he is "Messiah" or "Christ," and that on several occasions. This abrupt blurting out of such information is highly suspect. Either Mark or John is mistaken. We think it is John.

This gospel omits the "Temptation" story completely. John has a decided tendency to elevate the divinity of Jesus far above his humanity, and it would appear that John's redactors were unwilling to write of a true temptation event in which Jesus may have actually been able to sin!

Though John places the "Cleansing of the Temple" at the beginning of Jesus' ministry, and the synoptics place it at the end, no one need believe that Jesus cleansed it twice. John seems not to understand the symbolism of the act, whereby Jesus is preparing

PART TWO . . . in which I turn to the Bible

the things of God for the new and sovereign reign and coming kingdom. John's recounting is clearly out of place.

There is no "Upper Room and Last Supper" scene. Jesus' foot washing predominates. There are some very strange verses about eating Jesus' flesh and drinking his blood earlier in John 6. Since there is no appropriate context for this saying, it appears very odd and curious. Whatever the editors knew about the Last Supper, these verses do not describe it.

John also omits the "Garden of Gethsemane" agony. Jesus' "drops of blood" and the horror of approaching death do not appear. They give way to the formal, controlled, so called "High Priestly Prayer." The end of that beautiful soliloquy leads immediately to Jesus' arrest. Again, were the editors uncomfortable with the all-too-human Jesus of this dramatic scene?

After the resurrection, John writes of Jesus' seaside encounter, with the focus on Peter's rehabilitation. There is, however, no commissioning of the disciples for ministry in the world, unless Jesus' breathing on them in chapter 20 is an equivalent act.

There is, too, no "Ascension" scene. We are left with only some revealing editorial comments about how many books could be filled with Jesus' words and deeds if only someone would gather them all and take the time to write them down. From this presumed wealth of available materials, why did John's redactors leave out of their gospel so much that was right before them? How did they decide? Where did all this treasure trove end up? Did such material really exist, or is this statement simple, harmless exaggeration?

This is not intended as a commentary on John's gospel. I write to indicate why the gospel is not part of the study of Jesus and eternal torment. Though we are very sure that the "School of John" believed in eternal hell (see the book of Revelation), we can safely report that John's gospel does not teach that doctrine in any graphic or explicit language. It does not use the word Gehenna. Since we accept the scholarly conclusions about the Johannine authorship of 1, 2, 3 John, and the Revelation, we will save our brief remarks about those books for later, even as we remember how full of hell and torment is this last book in our Bibles.

John's Gospel

There are verses to consider, however, in John's gospel presentation. Truly, Jesus speaks of entering judgment, of wooden branches being tossed into the fire. These words can be literal enough without reference to real persons going to torment. The Jews he calls "children of the Devil." This is figurative, by any account, though harsh judgement of Jews is pronounced throughout.

John 3:16, the most famous New Testament verse, states that whoever believes in the son should not perish but have everlasting life. What does "perish" mean? Since the Greek word is used in other places to mean "lost," many believe the best translation is, ". . .whoever believes will not be lost." The same word appears in Matthew 15 and Luke 15. Both verses are translated "lost" sheep. Eternal hell seems not to be the meaning of John 3:16's warning.

Furthermore, in John 3:36, twenty verses later, Jesus is quoted: "whoever believes in the son has eternal life, but anyone who does not believe will not see life, but the wrath of God is on him."

John is highly comfortable with Jesus' constant self-reference as the saving one, "the son." There are many other Johannine images for Jesus, such as door, vine, gate, way, truth, life, etc. None of these appear in the synoptics. They are all reminiscent of the "I Am" statements in the Old Testament, using the exact words found in the ancient Hebrew scriptures called the Septuagint. Therein, "I Am" is quoting God Almighty. In John's gospel, it seems, Jesus is claiming to be equivalent with God. "Believing in the Son" is believing in God-as-the-Son. Not believing brings down God's wrath which negates "life."

The whole concept of "life" in John's gospel is a many-faceted subject. To relate the exact meaning of every usage in every verse requires extremely diligent exegesis by Johannine scholars. Even then, many questions remain.

These things: if John 3:36 is about eternal torment, sustained by God's wrath, then God will be unhappily wrathful for all eternity. That is logically unthinkable. Also, in other New Testament scriptures, God's wrath is certainly recognized. But it is not a part of his "personality" which must be reconciled with his more gentle, loving self. Wrath is situationally reactive, not a permanent

PART TWO . . . in which I turn to the Bible

response. An eternally rage-filled divinity is more like Greek and Roman gods than anything we read about in the Bible.

If an eternal hell was created and exists to appease the wrath of God, we have an interesting dilemma: God's wrath will never be satisfied, for hell will burn forever. Furthermore, and even more troubling, is the notion that if, after a while, God's wrath is appeased but she allows the punishment in torment to continue forever, we have monumental concerns about the moral-ethical character of God. The Bible is filled with texts about judgment for very same thing—the lack of human concern for the suffering and pain of others. How does this fundamental teaching apply to an indifferent diety overseeing the agony and cry of untold millions of his own creatures?

When we ponder John's insistence that "Jesus is God" we have linguistic and theological problems galore. For example, John 1:14: "And the Word became flesh. . .," cannot be literally true. If thought to be so, it can lead to all kinds of linguistic and philosophical confusion. We have a savior who is a man in appearance only. He "seems" to be human, but is, in fact, God. This kind of theology led to the early church heresy of Docetism. It denies the significance of the "flesh" of Jesus, strongly over-emphasizing the divinity. John, as we have seen, has a pronounced predisposition to lean in this direction. A too heavy focus on his gospel has always led the church into unhealthy waters.

John, then, must be "watered down" and interpreted in the light of the synoptics. It cannot be the other way around without our losing the historical Jesus in a cloudy mist of phantom-worship. For centuries the church dealt aggressively with defining the person and work of Jesus, thereby creating its Christology. John's gospel has always presented thorny problems in this sometimes divisive endeavor. That work goes on.

An authentic utterance of Jesus about universal redemption appears in John 12:32. It demands a thoughtful discussion here. John's writers have a strong tendency to "read the mind" of Jesus. The fact that they do this, on numerous occasions, gives helpful insight into how this gospel was written. The editors felt quite free to do so, certain that they had intuited Jesus' meaning for all to read. In many verses, John's writers say that Jesus "knew" this or that; he "meant" this or that. They had, of course, no access to the inner workings of Jesus' mind, but they were beyond bold in their efforts at clairvoyance.

The most remarkable instance of this relates to the theme of all these essays. In John 12:32, Jesus is quoted: "And I, if I am lifted up, will draw all persons unto myself." The editors must have been highly discomfited by this most obvious declaration of universal salvation. And since they "just knew" Jesus could not be talking about God's activity to save all persons through Jesus, despite his plainly saying so, John's redactors tell us what Jesus was really thinking. He was simply talking about his death on a cross! (v.33)

But even that enlargement will not do, for the writers deal only with, "If I am lifted up. . ." We can all grasp that Jesus was possibly speaking of his being lifted up on a cross, a common Roman form of execution. But even Jesus could not know that for sure. John's editors would know that after the fact, of course. But they do not deal with the phrase, "I will draw all to myself."

Since these scribes believed in a fiery, eternal hell, to them Jesus could not possibly have meant that a universal redemption was related to his life and death. It appears that they did not understand, therefore, that this plain declaration was about that precisely.

The work of the redactors on John 12:32 is a perfect example of editorial comment completely distorting the meaning of what must be a quite genuine saying. The true meaning lay right on the surface; their presuppositions precluded their grasping it. Their theology did not match that of Jesus!

Jesus speaks this verse out of his self-understanding found in the Servant Poems of Isaiah. He may well be quoting Isaiah 52:13, "See, my servant shall prosper; he shall be lifted up and shall be very high." The 53rd chapter is the most obvious scripture to ascertain Jesus' servant mission. 53:12 declares, "he poured himself out to death," and "he bore the sins of many." "Many" here in Isaiah is, of course, "all" in its parallelism.

PART TWO . . . in which I turn to the Bible

We now leave John's gospel with Jesus still by the sea, talking to his disciples. Unless we are missing another ending due to manuscript corruption, this is it. From the sweeping, profoundly magnificent Prologue in chapter 1, we regrettably must console ourselves with this puzzling, drab, even disappointing ending. John's scribes claim that much, much more material—enough to fill the whole world with books—was right at their fingertips. Why was it not used? So few answers!

Paul
Hell Yes; Hell No

FROM THE PRINTING FORMAT of our modern New Testaments, one might get the impression that the four gospels were written first. One might even get the notion that other writers of scripture had access to these gospels as resources for their own compositions. Nothing could be further from the truth.

The dating of the New Testament books remains a matter of some controversy and conjecture. It could not be otherwise, since the 27 texts are "ancient literature" and hard to place in a historical context. One common agreement among scholars is, however, that Paul wrote many of his books—perhaps all—before the gospels were circulated extensively. This is an extremely important concept as we reflect on all Christian theology, and particularly the doctrine of our concern, unending hell.

Where, then, did Paul obtain his information on the life and teachings of Jesus? He gives us clues enough to identify some of his sources. He openly declares that his life was changed through a personal appearance to him of Jesus, the Christ. After that incident, he isolated himself for three years in the area of Damascus, Syria, and was in fellowship with Christians there. He apparently imbibed the Syrian Christian teaching on the "end times," with its views of an eternal separation of the righteous and the unrighteous. Later, he returned to Jerusalem where he conferred with many disciples and apostles. He states that much of his knowledge was "handed to him," probably a reference to the sayings-deeds

PART TWO ... in which I turn to the Bible

materials on Jesus. These were oral and written, and in possession of Christian leaders wherever he went. Finally, he reported that he had "many revelations," experiences satisfactory to himself that they were directly from God, the Spirit, and/or Jesus Christ.

Even after these consultations, conversations, and visions, Paul shows little interest in what we would call "the historical Jesus." He writes nothing about the details of the earthly life of the Nazarene and says little about his sayings-deeds. He focuses squarely on the resurrection, attempting to indicate the world-changing significance of the "risen Christ." Sometimes, Paul's interpretations are correct. Sometimes, they are not. That study is not our topic here, however.

Paul's authority as an apostle was openly and aggressively questioned by many, but in time he was accounted the greatest of all interpreters of Christianity. Much that the church believes and teaches about its faith is solidly Pauline. One could say that Christianity is essentially Pauline, as supplemented, in time, by the gospels and other church literature. His influence as a historical figure is second only to Jesus himself.

With specific reference to our topic, the concept of unending torment, Paul's early teaching solidly embraced the Syrian Christian and Pharisaic Jewish view. His evolution in understanding and faith, on many topics, can be traced in his letters and epistles. Our position would be that by the time he wrote his masterwork, Romans, he believed wholeheartedly in universal redemption. He had become "persuaded" (Rom. 8:38) that nothing could separate anyone from the love of God in Jesus Christ. His great summary of all cosmic events is Romans 11:36: "For from Him and through Him and to Him are all things." Paul had become a committed universalist.

While there is scholarly disagreement about the authorship of several New Testament books, including some historically attributed to Paul, there is substantial agreement that he did, in fact, write Romans, 1 and 2 Corinthians, 1 and 2 Thessalonians, Galatians, Colossians, Philippians, and Philemon. Additionally, and importantly for interpreters, there is no concern that Paul's materials have been substantially "worked over" by scribes, editors, or redactors, as in the gospels. What we read today is essentially the same work written by the Apostle.

The story of the gathering of his books, their collection and ultimate inclusion in the canon is not our subject. While Paul's name as author was attached to some books thought to be his, scholarship over the years has reversed those decisions. While the historic figures who penned the books in question cannot be identified, the church has agreed that those other works are, indeed, appropriately placed among Christian scripture.

With Paul's words readily at hand, we can look to these several books to see if he taught eternal torment. We declare that he did, but then had a significant change in his theology, thereafter openly declaring the ultimate redemption of all through the agape love of God. In this exposition of his thoughts, Paul can almost "speak for himself."

1. FIRST AND SECOND THESSALONIANS

The order of Paul's writings is a matter of some dispute, but everyone agrees that these two letters are "early Paul."

In the first letter Paul does not explicitly say that anyone will be lost forever, but he does use language about the wrath of God coming upon sinners. "The Lord will punish all such sins..." (4:6). He writes of the Coming of the Lord but has no ominous judgment scene. Interestingly, even here he declares that God did not "appoint us to suffer wrath but to receive salvation..." (5:9).

Second Thessalonians picks up the Second Coming narrative with 1:7–9 declaring that Jesus will come in blazing fire punishing "those who do not know God and do not obey the gospel of our Lord Jesus." Then the punishment is explained: "everlasting destruction," and being shut out from the presence and majesty of his power.

Chapter 1:10 states that Christ will be glorified and marveled at among the believers. Not so among the others. Chapter 2:11–12 has never been satisfactorily explained: God will send a delusion

PART TWO . . . in which I turn to the Bible

so that some believe a lie, then they will be condemned for believing it!

Under what circumstances Paul rethought all this and reversed his opinions, we do not know. His letters are both personal and theological, but he makes no reference to the events surrounding the remarkable shift in his entire theological orientation. He does, gratefully, detail that change in relatively clear teaching thereafter. We find his universalism most transparently taught in his magnum opus, Romans, and also in several other books that he wrote and others that are attributed to him.

2. ROMANS

A cursory reading of Romans might lead one to conclude that the human race is "not worth saving!" The sin and degradation of persons is on full display in Paul's language analysis. Here is a very brief sampling of his assessment:

- 1:18 "The wrath of God is being revealed against all the godlessness and wickedness of those who suppress the truth by their wickedness."
- 1:29 "They have become filled with every kind of wickedness, evil, greed, and depravity."
- 2:5 "Because of your stubbornness and unrepentant heart, you are storing up wrath against yourself for the day of God's wrath."
- 2:9 "There will be trouble and distress for everyone who does evil."
- 3:9 "Jews and Gentiles alike are all under sin."
- 3:10 "There is no one righteous, not even one." 3:10–18 is his all-inclusive, devastating summary, quoting the Old Testament.

This catalog of verses could be expanded easily with several other citations from chapters 1–3. Everything turns at the end of chapter 3, as we shall see.

Even so, chapter 7 reveals the heartfelt corporate solidarity of the great apostle with his fellow human beings, for in that chapter he writes 19 verses about his own sin and struggle with the "sin nature." Paul writes about "us," not just "them."

After this remarkable, if humiliating dissection of all things human, Paul begins the slow turn toward his ultimate message: universal redemption. In 3:23-24, he declares that "all have sinned and fall short of the glory of God," and/but, "all are justified freely by his grace through the redemption that came through Jesus Christ." All have sinned; all are justified. This is an accomplished fact by divine decree, made before the foundation of the world. The working out of God's plan in the lives of the already redeemed will take the time it takes, but the outcome is a divinely ordained certainty.

Paul is just beginning his teaching on ultimate redemption. He thinks of the sin of Adam, in 5:15: "If the many (all) died by the trespass of one man (Adam), how much more did God's grace overflow to the many (all) in Jesus Christ."

He continues to think and write with Adam in mind. In 5:18 he declares that "as the result of one trespass (by Adam) condemnation came on all, by one act of righteousness (by Jesus) justification brings life for all." In 5:19 he concludes his thought: by the disobedience of one man (Adam) many (all) were made sinners, so through the obedience of one man (Jesus) the many (all) will be made righteous.

Paul's plain teaching will get even plainer as he goes on toward the rhapsodic chapter 11.

Chapter 6 contains various teachings, but two verses reflect the vectors of Paul's thought. Verse 10, he writes, "Christ died to sins once for all people." In verse 23, "the gift of God is eternal life in Christ Jesus our Lord." In chapter 7, he inquires about his own sin, and speaking for all, he asks in agony, "Who will deliver me from this body of death? Thanks be to God—Jesus Christ our Lord!"

Chapter 8 contains the wonderfully reassuring verses: what can separate us from the love of God in Christ? Nothing in all

PART TWO . . . in which I turn to the Bible

creation! Paul either means this or he does not. In Romans we must conclude that he is this adamant—nothing.

Chapter 9: 1 to 11:24 has spawned much erroneous and faulty theology. My only point is that if it is recognized that this section is about God's work in Jewish history, one will be in the correct place to interpret the material. Nothing is being said about the eternal destiny of anyone! To read into the text that these verses are about salvation or damnation in the afterlife is to misunderstand the subject entirely.

Paul does come back to eternal concerns in 11:25–36. After all this historical comment about the unfaithful Jews, he proclaims in verse 26: all Israel will be saved. How? Verse 29-32: God's gifts and call (decree) are irrevocable. God has bound over all (Jews and Gentiles) to disobedience so that he may have mercy on them all. At this, Paul cannot contain himself and he pens the universalist doxology:

"Oh, the depth of the riches of the wisdom and knowledge of God! How unsearchable his judgments, and his paths beyond tracing out. Who has known the mind of the Lord? Or who has been his counselor? Who has ever given to God that God should repay them. For from him and through him and for him are all things. To him be the glory forever! Amen." Verses 33–36

So, what are humans to do after hearing this dramatic presentation? Paul flips instantly into the "therefore" section of the book. At 12:1: Therefore, live your life in accordance with what you have just heard about your value to God, both here and hereafter. He says clearly, without stating it exactly like this: Remember, that "the other" is as precious to God as are you. Treat him or her accordingly. The ethical commands also have their cautions. In 14:10, Paul warns that we will all stand before God's judgment seat, and because of our actions we may endure God's "wrath." We cannot sin without consequence.

But at the judgment seat this comforting prospect: In 14:11, God says "as surely as I live, every knee will bow before me: every tongue will confess to God." There is no coercion here, nor mention of hearing, "Depart from me!" Verse 12 reminds that we will all give an open account of our lives to God. If this is a picture of our first day in eternity, remembering all we learn in Romans, it must be that God will then begin our preparation for eternally abiding in her holy presence. If we all experience wrath—and we will—we will ultimately experience the grace of the everlasting love, which can be overcome by nothing! So says Paul, the avowed Christian Universalist.

More Pauline Universalism

I WILL BRIEFLY REVIEW Paul's universalist comments in his other epistles.

1. 1 CORINTHIANS AND 2 CORINTHIANS

Millions believe that eternal hell and unending punishment are theological truths that punctuate and propel all things Christian. However, one looking for such concepts in the two letters to Corinth will be disappointed. That teaching is not there. Let me note a few things that are.

One, Paul believed that the Second Coming was imminent. Two, he believed that the dead were in "soul sleep" until roused at that Second Coming. Three, Paul attempted to present a rough chronology of the events following Christ's coming.

Paul's belief in the timing of Jesus' return is not crucially important and has been argued by scholars. The Thessalonian letters make it clear that, at that writing, he was looking skyward. Nothing in these Corinthian letters says exactly that, though in chapter 7, a long chapter with instructions for marriage, among other things, Paul states, "the time is short." This cryptic phrase could be used anytime, anywhere, of course. General admonitions to be morally alert are commonplace, and a favorite theme of Jesus' parables.

Paul did write in clear language that the dead are in the grave. Again, the two Thessalonian letters make his view explicit, even as 6:14 and 15:52 do here. 6:14 states that "God raised the Lord from

More Pauline Universalism

the dead and will raise us also." 15:52 is clearer: "at the last trump the dead will be raised." While Paul may have changed his mind by the writing of 2 Corinthians, he teaches soul sleep here. (see 2 Corinthians 5:8)

The apostle gives a highly significant outline of the unfolding of events when the Second Coming finally occurs. The outline is this (15:20–28): Christ is the "first fruits" of the dead and when he comes he will raise those "who belong to him." Then Christ will reign until he has destroyed "all dominion, authority and power," including death, the "last enemy." He rules until everything is put under his feet, then gives the Kingdom to "God the Father." At that time, God will be all in all. In this sequence, events positively cannot happen instantaneously. Paul's words are "then, when" (v.23), "then," (v.24), "when" (v.28). We can well ask what are the "periods of time" in this chronology, and what does it mean that Christ "overcomes" all evil? In several essays below, I propose answers related to what must take place for all souls to be saved eternally. But two earlier 1 Corinthians passages are certainly to be "plugged in" to this Pauline timeframe.

One is 3:15, the concluding verse about foundations built on anything other than Jesus Christ: that work will be shown for what it is, because the day will bring it to light. So, a man has lived his life and organized his world around gold, silver, costly jewels, wood, hay, or straw. What of him when his "work" is exposed? "He will be saved, as one escaping through the flames." (v.15) Paul is clear and Paul is certain.

The other passage refers to the man committing sexual, social sins. What to do with him? 5:5: "Hand him over to Satan, so that the sinful nature may be destroyed and his spirit saved on the Day of the Lord."

Are these two examples of what Christ accomplishes in order to "destroy" evil power at his second coming, the Day of the Lord? It seems apparent.

The terms "fire" and "Satan" can be debated, but if Paul intends what he says, in plain language, we have the most challenging idea of turning a sinner over to this fire and this Satan, for a kind of disciplinary rehabilitation. What is not debatable is Paul's two strong conclusion statements: "he himself will be saved," and "his spirit may be saved" on that day.

In this chronology of the end time, Paul missed the most obvious of opportunities to include an ominous Judgment Day scene, leading to an eternal and fiery hell. Why, indeed? Because he did not believe in eternal torment. He believed that sinners could and would be saved, by whatever means, through agape love acting in the interim period between Christ's return and God being all in all. Neither 1 nor 2 Corinthians makes mention of a place of unending suffering.

2. GALATIANS

There is no reference to life after death and ultimate outcomes in this book. In chapter 1, Paul does write that the curse of God shall be on anyone who perverts the gospel. Calling down God's wrath is not condemning to eternal torment, however.

In chapter 5, Paul shares a long list of sinful acts and declares that those who live this way will not inherit the Kingdom of God. This is a "warning" (v.21) as he says, indicating that in God's presence no sin will be allowed its contaminating influence. Those who belong to Christ must live by the Spirit and acquire the "fruit of the Spirit" for godly living. I will revisit the theme of God disallowing sin in her heaven. We cannot imagine that any sin listed in chapter 5 would or could be found in a perfect eternal realm.

3. PHILIPPIANS

I use this statement for yet another Pauline letter: there is no mention here of a place of unending torment and pain. Two passages deserve a brief note, however.

One is the "Philippian Hymn," as it is called, of 2:6–11. Paul does not appear to be its author; he seems to be quoting something already known to these church members. He writes that the hymn gives a glimpse into the mind and attitude of Christ, which attitude should be in the Philippians. The hymn's conclusion is this: God exalted Christ and gave him a name above every name, that at his name "ever knee should bow in heaven, on earth, and under the earth." And every tongue should "confess that Jesus is Lord."

These words mirror Old Testament passages found in Psalm 110 and Isaiah 45. Paul had used the same language in Romans 14:11. The hymn writers' appropriation of those passages is now translated into the acknowledgement of universal redemption through Jesus Christ.

Is this ancient affirmation about force and power, or about grateful obedience? Will God slam the mass of sinful humanity to its knees, or will humanity willingly praise Christ in its awareness that salvation has come for all?

This may be the most ancient hymn in the history of the Christian church. It hardly seems likely that the closing lines were intended to crush and humiliate non-believers in Christ. It seems very likely that they intend ultimate praise and celebration, as all, everyone, acknowledges this redemption through the agape love of God in Christ.

The very idea of a diety forcing terrified, screaming sinners to acknowledge that he was right, with a "See, I told you so!" before forcing them into an eternal hell of fire, is both morally repugnant and contrary to everything known about the God of Jesus.

In 3:12, Paul offers a welcome comment about the evolution into holiness: "Not that I have already been made perfect, but I press on. . ." This certainly reminds all that Christian maturity is a slow process, requiring experience in overcoming temptation and in doing good. Paul adds in verse 16: "Let us live up to what we have already attained."

4. COLOSSIANS

A couple of passages in this short book are clear indicators of Paul's belief in salvation for all, and how it will be accomplished.

PART TWO . . . in which I turn to the Bible

Chapter 1 relates how God's fullness dwells in Christ, and that through him all things will be reconciled to himself. (v.19,20). Verse 17 is a curious, enlightening verse: In Christ, all things "hold together."

In chapter 2, Paul states that by the cross, God "disarmed" the hostile, militant "powers and authorities" (then back to 1:20) "reconciling them and making peace." This passage may be usefully compared to Paul's end time chronology in 1 Corinthians 15, mentioned above.

It is difficult to believe that anyone would use the term "peace" when thinking that all opposing persons and forces were to end in eternal suffering and torment. Paul does not believe that. 3:15 reads, "you were called to peace."

Thus, we see that in the authentic Pauline literature the apostle never says that anyone will go to an unending torment, nor that just one person is suffering there now. If any affirm that about Paul's teaching, they must "explain away" a multitude of verses which plainly teach otherwise.

Six Universalist Writings

I MAINTAIN THAT EPHESIANS, 1 and 2 Timothy, Titus, and 1 and 2 Peter teach universal salvation directly. I also maintain that James teaches it by indirection.

1. JAMES

There is nothing in this book which is incompatible with universal redemption. He, of course, does not "come right out and say it." He does say that "the Judge is at the door," (5:9), but then quickly adds in 5:11, "you have seen the purpose of the Lord (the Judge), how he is compassionate and merciful." This Judge's decisions are made on the basis of agape love for all who appear before him. If that is indeed the mindset of the coming God, then saving someone from "death" is as paramount for the merciful Judge—God as it is for the merciful disciple attempting to bring one sinner back (5:20). Can God be less concerned over wayward sinners than the unnamed Christian commended for saving one from "death," thereby "covering a multitude of sins" (5:19–20)? Does James believe that if a sinner is not brought back, he will burn eternally? That seems completely out of line with the overall teaching of his book.

He could have elaborated on the wrathful outcome for those who did not adequately prepare for what he believed was imminent: "the Lord is at hand" (5:8). He could have written dire warnings to the many, rather than use the poignant and tender reference to "one sinner." He does not. In 1:18, remembering what

PART TWO . . . in which I turn to the Bible

he will write later about the Lord's return, he states that the first century disciples, ("we"), are a kind of "first fruits" of salvation. Will the harvest be over when Christ returns on any given day? Will God, as compassionate and merciful, continue the harvest? The alternative would be simply that "soon the harvest is past," and untold millions will be cast into unending torment. The tone and tenor of the book dictate against such a ghastly outcome.

All students of James have paused upon reading the verse at 3:6: "the tongue also is a fire. . ., sets the whole course of one's life on fire, and is itself set on fire by hell." The "hell" is the Greek word, Gehenna, and is certainly figurative. This is clearly not a comment about any existing place, but appears in a long section on self control. The emphasis is on monitoring one's language and speaking in concert with one's faith.

This is the only New Testament usage of Gehenna outside the synoptic gospels. There is no logical relationship between the fires of an eternal hell and the human tongue. We understand the implied relationship, however, when the tongue produces in speech that which is foul and vulgar. Saying that something is "straight out of hell" is common enough.

James is another writer of New Testament literature who simply does not appear to think that the salvation of souls turns on a definable criterion, absent which fiery dread awaits. He writes what later editors have divided into five chapters and never says anything of the kind. He did not believe it, I am convinced.

2. THE PASTORAL EPISTLES

Those who believe in eternal torment must scramble when reading the so-called Pastoral Epistles. In order to maintain their belief in a vengeful God who damns eternally, they must state that these letters "do not say" what they clearly say! The key verses are these: 1 Timothy 2:3-6; 4:10; Titus 2:11. Second Timothy does not deal with the subject of eternal endings, but should be read in conjunction with the other two epistles.

1 Timothy 2:3–6 reads: "God our Savior wills that all be saved and come to the knowledge of the truth. For there is one God, and there is one mediator between God and humanity, the man Christ Jesus, who gave himself a ransom for all."

These points seem irrefutable: "all" means "all" in these verses. The writer, probably not Paul, is reflecting Jesus' language in Mark 10:45, "the Son of Man came to give his life as a ransom for many." That language is Jesus' recalling of the Servant Poem in Isaiah 53:11, ". . . my righteous servant shall justify many." There, of course, Isaiah repeatedly uses "many" for "all." Also, in Timothy's verse 2, "God wills. . ." all to be saved. The Greek word for "will" must be studied carefully, for it does not mean that, "God hopes it is so," or "God would like for it to be so." This word describes God's eternal intent to redeem all. I equate this with a divine decree that all persons will come to the saving knowledge, mentioned here (v.4).

1 Timothy 4:10, is classic universalism's most unassailable verse. "We have set our hope on the living God, who is the Savior of all, especially of those who believe." There is no other way to read or interpret this verse than as it states in its obvious simplicity. "All" is a category distinct from "those who believe." Who, then, is left out of this saving work of God? No one.

This verse focuses entirely on God's action. It must, of course, be understood as the work of God-in-Christ. "Those who believe" savingly believe now. When will the rest of "all humanity" come to believe? In God's good time.

Titus 2:11 states, "The grace of God has appeared for the salvation of all." As a text in this third Pastoral Epistle, it reiterates the thought of 1 Timothy with its unequivocal universalism.

3. FIRST AND SECOND PETER

First and Second Peter present unique understandings of the operation of God's love in the salvation of all.

In 1 Peter 3:19–20, God's grace toward even the shameless and disobedient souls "in prison" suddenly appears through Jesus

Christ. Why would God bother to do that? So that though "judged in the flesh like human beings," they might "live in the spirit like God" (4:6). The author does not diminish or dismiss the depth of sin in anyone, but he is confident that in the final judgment before God and Christ, they will receive this unwarranted mercy (4:5-6). Verse 8 proclaims that "love covers a multitude of sins." This writer thinks that it truly covers sins both in this world and the next. The souls "in prison" are already dead!

2 Peter 3:9 declares that God does not want anyone to perish, but wants everyone to come to repentance. The Greek word here is all-important for defining God's intention. Though different from the word in 1 Timothy 2:4, it must necessarily mean that this "wanting" is God's absolute decision to save. Again, it has nothing to do with God's whim or fond wishes. It is an affirmation in power declaring that God decrees it so eternally. Had the Greek words here and in 1 Timothy 2 been properly translated through the years, belief in universalism would have been more decidedly acknowledged as the doctrine around which all Christian theology revolves. It is time to reclaim it as such. All creatures will be saved, not because God fervently hopes it, but because God declares it so.

4. EPHESIANS

The authorship of this book remains uncertain, but whoever penned it was perfectly clear about final outcomes in the ages to come. The pertinent passages are as beautiful as they are instructive.

1:10: God will "bring all things in heaven and on earth together under one head, even Christ." 1:22-23: God placed all things under the feet of Christ and appointed him to be head of the Church, which is "the fullness of him who fills everything in every way."

This book contains several verses about the "good pleasure," "will," "mystery," and "plan" of God, decrees occurring before the foundation of the world. There is clearly predestination here: God purposed to bring all things together under one head—Christ (1:10). This mystery has been made known to the writer (3:3), and through him to the readers (3:4). What was veiled in unknowing is now revealed in light: God through Christ will save all. God's plan to redeem has begun with the appearance of Jesus Christ, and in the coming ages God will show us all the "incomparable riches of her grace." (2:7). We are God's workmanship (2:10). Will God allow his holy work to fail in its purpose and goal? No, he will not! Would God begin and then not complete?

No Hell In Acts

THE CHRISTIAN CHURCH HAS generally recognized that Luke's Book of Acts contains some historically factual material about the spread of the church. Jesus' commissioning of disciples led some of them, after his ascension, to begin the arduous effort of proclaiming among the people of the Middle East the profound significance of his life and teaching. It took some time, and sharp controversy, for the disciples to accept the fact that the story of Jesus was to also be shared with "Gentiles." I suspect that the conversion of Paul, to be minister among non-Jews, is told three times in Acts for this reason.

It is important to our task to ask, "What was the tone, tenor, and content of the message the disciples proclaimed in Acts?" Was their main thrust to "save people from the fires of unending torment?" Absolutely not! This was not their "gospel" at all. (It is quite worthwhile to go through the New Testament defining the term "gospel" as it appears. There are multiple definitions throughout.)

We need not examine every sermon and narrative in Acts in order to make our point. We can analyze a couple of passages for confirmation.

In Acts 2, Peter preaches the first sermon in the new Christian church. It would appear that his message ought to be about salvation from eternal hell. It is not. He does not give an emotional call, encouraging hearers to "accept Jesus Christ." In fact, the audience asks him what they should do, since they were now convinced of their collective guilt in crucifying Jesus. His response is, "Repent

No Hell In Acts

and be baptized." In verse 40, Peter concludes his admonition: "Save yourselves from this crooked, corrupt generation." He does not say, "Save yourselves from everlasting hell."

Peter preaches again in chapter 3. He gives moral and ethical demands, never mentioning eternal doom. He does, however, speak one of the most intriguing utterances in the New Testament. In 3:20–21 Luke records Peter's words: "... Jesus ... must remain in heaven until the time of universal restoration that God announced long ago through his holy prophets."

There has not been scholarly agreement on the meaning of this Greek term, apokatastasis, "universal restoration." Opinions vary widely. But the case can certainly be made for comparing this verse with several others in the Epistles which clearly teach universal salvation as universal restoration of all things. (Rom. 11:36, 1 Cor. 15:28, Eph. 1:10, Col. 1:20)

In this long New Testament book there are many other instances of an evangelist confronting a non-believing audience. These speakers include Stephen, Phillip, Peter, and Paul. In not one recorded account are hearers told to accept Jesus or be consigned to eternal torment. That is, quite simply, not the subject of any sermon in Acts.

Sheer logic should inform one who believes in eternal hell that the earliest preaching in Christian history should mirror preaching in these our days: the focus must surely be on saving the lost from perdition. No such content can be found in Luke's Book of Acts. The conclusion that such a doctrine was not an essential feature of first century preaching would be unquestionably correct. No other is available. No word from any audience of Christians, no comment at all, reflects their joy and relief at being snatched from the jaws of an unending, fiery abyss. Comparisons with today's urgings to avoid hell seem urgently and necessarily indicated!

85

The Minority
Eternal Hell

SINCE THE BIBLE IS not uniform in its messaging, it is not difficult for universalists to acknowledge that some books in the New Testament plainly teach eternal hell. It would be gratifying if those who adhered to that doctrine would at least concede that some New Testament books plainly teach universal redemption. But arriving at that point would presuppose the concurrence of a number of events which seem unlikely to unfold.

Even so, the numbers add up to what may be a concerning fact for those advocating eternal torment. The truth is this: early Paul, the Matthew School, Luke, Mark, the Johannine School, the Epistle to the Hebrews, and the Epistle of Jude are the only books which teach an eternal fiery doom. John's gospel is not transparent in proclaiming it, and the three epistles of John cannot be claimed to teach the doctrine on the basis of the plain content of the existing texts. Only as part of the Joannine tradition can it be affirmed that the teaching is implied. Clearly, however, the Book of Revelation teaches it as included in the corpus from John's scribes. Hebrews and Jude can be read in no other way.

There are twenty-seven books in the New Testament. Eight books clearly teach unending doom. This minority grouping must be declared the interpretive key to the other nineteen in order for eternal torment to be declared the correct and only teaching of the New Testament. That argument is tendentious at best, and clearly subject to contrarian views and discussion.

There is no need to reproduce here the pertinent texts from the books universally agreed to propose everlasting woe. However, some comments about a few of their verses seems warranted, even necessary. I have previously dealt with the gospel of John, and in an upcoming essay I explore the synoptic gospel texts about hell and torment. Here, I will address a few points of concern about Hebrews and Revelation.

Hebrews 6:4–6 identifies one avenue which leads to "eternal Judgment" (v.2). The writer claims that it is impossible to bring to repentance those who have once been enlightened, tasted the heavenly gift, shared in the Holy Spirit, and tasted the goodness of God's word, if they "fall away." Hebrews 10:26 presents another route to hell. For those who deliberately "keep on sinning," no sacrifice for sin is left.

It is patently true, and observable from ordinary human behavior, that some people lose any interest in things spiritual, even after a long "career" of faithfulness. Certainly, some choose to continue in all kinds of sin. But it is patently false that any person reaches a "point of no return" in this life, from which forgiveness is no longer offered or available. Such a view is contrary to human experience, and clearly violates the transparent teaching of most of the New Testament—especially that of Jesus. Universalism goes much further by declaring that even if forgiving grace is spurned in this life, it will still be available and ultimately effectively applied in the life to come.

I am quite sure that the author of this odd Book of Hebrews, whoever it was, believed in eternal damnation. Too many verses attest to that fact. Even so, he comes close, time and again, to offering God's love to all persons for all eternity. But, he cannot quite allow himself to do it. Even so, he makes comment after comment on God's reaction to sin and her solution to its eradication in time and eternity.

Despite his beliefs about hell, he leaves us with some of the most profound words in the entire New Testament. For my purposes in this essay, these are memorable.

PART TWO . . . in which I turn to the Bible

10:31: "It is a fearful, dreadful thing to fall into the hands of the living God." Yet, we all shall.

10:39: "But we are not of those who shrink back," despite knowing we will meet God.

12:6: Quoting Proverbs 3, "The Lord disciplines those he loves and punishes everyone he accepts as a child." And we all are children of her love.

12:10: "God disciplines us for our good, that we may share in his holiness." This is the confident faith of Christian universalism.

12:11: "No discipline seems pleasant at the time, but pain." It cannot be easy for us sinners to be cleansed from all our sin for all eternity.

12:11: "But discipline produces peace for those who have been trained by it." Peace is coming to all in God's good time, universalism proclaims.

12:14: "Without holiness, no one will see the Lord." Who would want to stand before God clinging to their sin? Then we must be made holy, for our heart's deepest desire is to see the living God, and to be with God forever.

Let us now join the writers of the Book of Revelation, imagining the scene where myriads of human creatures are writhing in agony and unspeakable suffering. As we contemplate this, what is our response to the horror we perceive?

Curiously, there is a Biblical response to that very distressing scene. In chapter 14, we see a fiery hell in full, flourishing operation. Verse 11 says: "And the smoke of their pain, suffering, torment and torture goes up forever and forever." That is the reality being observed by the writer. But there is an additional audience. Verse 10 says those in hell will be tormented with hot, burning sulfur in the presence of the holy angels and of the Lamb, Jesus Christ. But there are more to view it. In chapter 19 we learn that the spectators watching the awful suffering are not only John, Jesus, and the holy angels. No! The writer says that, "I heard what sounded like a tumultuous roar from the multitudes in heaven" (v.1). So, what is the visceral,

The Minority

emotional response, from all those viewing it, to this frightening scene? The writer informs us. They were literally shouting with glee. Verse 3 tells us why: Again they roared their approval saying, "Hallelujah! The smoke of hell goes up forever and ever." And verse 7: "Let us rejoice and be glad, and give God glory."

And there we have it! Everyone there enjoying and applauding the shrieking agony of the lost in hell. It is a highly acceptable scene and show to the spectators and audience, in John's Revelation, of things that must soon come to pass (1:1).

This is a dark and deeply disturbing portion of scripture. We react to it with many emotions, no doubt. But if anything about the teaching of Jesus is remembered, rejoicing at the pain and suffering of others is certainly a sin. If anything is remembered about the teaching of the apostle Paul, and much of the New Testament, such a gleeful response to the agony of others is known to be a sin. If anything is remembered about the "God of Love," it is crystal clear that glorying in the sad, horrific misfortune of anyone is a sin.

What, then, about the Book of Revelation, and this spectacle? These unfortunate verses are simply not of Christ! They are unchristian!

One may believe in eternal hell, but to declare that those in heaven ought to clap and sing as others writhe is sadistic at best. Does God bless this behavior? She does not.

Rejoicing and praising God through and because of the pain, suffering, even death of others is a regular feature of Old Testament history. The concept of God evolved to a more humane point, culminating in the revelation of God's love and grace in the life and teaching of Jesus of Nazareth. The school of John was well aware of this, having penned the profound verse, "God is love" (1 John 4:8). Why the collective group of scribes reverted to such Old Testament-like scenes of gratuitous gore and carnage is unfortunate. Much of the Book of Revelation does nothing to help define the coming kingdom and the reign of love.

These challenging verses do force an intellectual and emotional answer to several questions, however. For those believing in fiery doom, how respond to the fact that millions including many

PART TWO . . . in which I turn to the Bible

known to, and perhaps loved by, the living, are now forever enchained in the dungeon of unrelenting misery? And, how do the "dead in heaven" respond to the same obvious fact? These questions have not been adequately addressed in church history. There is an understandable sheepishness when the issues are raised. But understandable or not, they are legitimate questions and issues at the very core of fundamental Christian perspective.

In psychoanalytic thought there is a defense mechanism called "identification with the aggressor." It is an unconscious process whereby someone adopts and takes on the mindset and behavior of a more powerful person than one's self. That could be any aggressor, abuser, torturer, bully, captor, and so on. It is a mechanism whereby one justifies one's behavior toward the object of aggression, absolving the self of the act of creating or inflicting the pain, suffering, or even death. Any personal guilt is thereby removed as the self is deemed to have committed no offense, error, evil, or, in religious terms, sin.

I believe this concept is highly relevant to the thinking process of those who espouse unending torment. If, in fact, God approves of eternal hell, then how can the "true believer" not do so as well? How can she or he not identify with the Lord God in the consignment of untold millions to their well-deserved doom? And how can this unending punishment not register some sense of satisfaction with the believer, since it is part and parcel of God's predetermined plan for how to deal with abject sinners and their sin?

While I hope that few will gleefully relish the contemplation of millions of souls in unending torment, the visceral reaction to this supposed reality must be analyzed carefully by its proponents. That is a psychological task well worth undertaking, but an even more important spiritual task. Christians must, of course, attempt to have in them" the mind of Christ," as Paul declared (Phil. 2:5–8). That odd phrase must surely mean that followers do their best to think as Jesus thought, even toward those perceived as enemies, adversaries, even those inflicting pain or causing insult. These are hard sayings, and few Christians achieve this rarified air in their discipleship. Nevertheless, it is commanded by Paul and by Jesus.

Many use the Book of Revelation to loudly proclaim that God will deal mercilessly with sin and sinners, consigning them to the misery of a fiery, eternal perdition. Universalists declare that truly God will destroy sin, but that God will save the sinner. That is a fact to produce unbounded joy!

Jesus Did Not Teach Eternal Hell

I HAVE STATED THAT as the "Son" of the God of agape love, Jesus of Nazareth did not believe in nor teach the doctrine of eternal torment. I have affirmed that the New Testament verses implying that he did so teach are the product of scribes, editors, and redactors who were his followers, but who created this picture of Jesus innocently and without deceptive intention.

It is now my task to examine the verses in question and in so doing to demonstrate the plausibility of what I am asserting here. I will review the sayings from the synoptic gospels with the reminder of the heavy emphasis on this teaching in Matthew, ten passages, with one in Luke and one in Mark. I have noted that I think this is a highly significant fact, vitally important for interpretive purposes.

In the analysis that follows, I am not declaring that any passage here is an authentic utterance of Jesus. We simply cannot know that. I am saying that, even if they are authentic, they warrant a new interpretive effort, since Jesus did not believe in, nor teach, unending torment. It is not intellectual honesty to saddle him with such an anti-agape doctrine.

The Greek word "Gehenna" has Aramaic and Hebrew roots, and is the term uniformly translated "hell" in the New Testament. There are only eight Gehenna sayings in the synoptics attributed to Jesus, and four additional verses in which he is quoted as teaching an eternal, fiery doom. The eight Gehenna hell passages appear in the texts as follows: Matthew 5:21–22, Matthew 5:27–30, Matthew

10:28, Matthew 18:8–9, Matthew 23:15, Matthew 23:33, Mark 9:43–50, Luke 12:4–5

Four other Matthew passages are said to teach eternal hell: Matthew 7:19, Matthew 13:36–43, Matthew 13:47–50, Matthew 25:30–46.

These are points to ponder as we begin.

1. The verse distribution and ratio indicate the strong focus on apocalyptic and endtime matters from the Matthew editors.
2. Thus, we see that Luke and Mark are obviously far less interested in commenting upon the dire fate of persons than is Matthew. There are no other verses in either of these two gospels about the woeful end of world events or eternal damnation.
3. This fact is crucially important. Three of the Gehenna passages are clearly from the same source. Matthew 5:29–30, Matthew 18:8–9, and Mark 9:43–50 all contain essentially identical sayings. There is only a slight variation, which I will note. Why the Matthew scribes placed this saying in Jesus' mouth twice is unknown.
4. Two additional sayings are also nearly identical. Matthew 10:28 and Luke 12:4–5 are definitely from common source material.
5. Matthew places two sayings from John the Baptist in the mouth of Jesus. Matthew 7:19, a non-Gehenna utterance, is John's language from Matthew 3:10. Matthew 23:33 is from John's words in Matthew 3:7. However, Matthew makes a change in vocabulary in the second instance. He modifies John's words, "coming wrath," to have Jesus say, "Gehenna." This is completely in line with Matthew's end time concerns.
6. Despite the common source material for all three synoptics, seven Matthew Gehenna eternal fire sayings have no parallels in Mark or Luke.

PART TWO . . . in which I turn to the Bible

Before the passages analysis, these additional comments are necessary.

1. No one knows for certain what Jesus did or did not do.
2. No one knows for certain what Jesus did or did not say.
3. All our information about these matters is contained in four gospels, three of which are under consideration here. The Gospel of John and other writings from outside our canon are not relevant to this inquiry, though Gehenna hell does not appear in John.
4. No human saying or action is uninterpreted.
5. No saying or action of Jesus is uninterpreted.
6. Every analysis of a saying-deed is based upon the presuppositions of the one commenting.
7. Presuppositions can be stated, generally speaking.
8. There are several sets of presupposition at work in any comment upon the sayings-deeds of Jesus.
9. For purposes of the essay, I can state that the presupposition of all three synoptic gospel editors is that Jesus believed in and taught eternal torment.
10. My fundamental presupposition, stated again, is that Jesus neither believed in nor taught unending doom.
11. My interpretive methodology for reading the text and reaching conclusions is this: synoptic study must be undertaken using the available tools of higher and lower criticism. Some of my conclusions related to this appeared in previous essays. Additional ones follow here.

If one accepts the fact that a vast amount of "Jesus material" was extant in the first century, and that our gospels are the result of intentional editorial work, then we come away with the obvious conclusion: the editors were comfortable and satisfied with the Jesus they presented to the world. They incorporated certain materials and discarded others, as their free editorial and scribal choice.

These writers, redactors, and editors thereby chose to depict Jesus in their own individual way. Why else would they write if not to preserve their own view and ideas about Jesus? That is what writers do. They had no idea or concept that their own gospel, nor any others, would be elevated to the status of holy writ in the emerging Christian community.

I say again that the Gospel of John, and some other non-canonical gospels, present a very different Jesus from the Jesus of the synoptics. A great deal of common material appears in all three synoptics, but very little of that material can be found in or ferreted out of John. This is witness to the freedom felt by John's editors to lean heavily on interpreting their material at the expense of recording historical fact. They take this approach even as they state that they have access to vast amounts of Jesus material.

Unavoidably, then, as human gospel writers, these ancient people overlay their presuppositions onto the sayings-deeds of Jesus. They naturally offer social, literary, and theological comments to match or reinforce their own predetermined conclusions. They did not write gospels looking for new insights into the significance of the life of Jesus. Neither were they "studying scripture;" they were creating it, unbeknownst to them, of course.

In fact, their presuppositions can be detected in how they organize and collate the material in the first place. Their ideas and convictions can certainly be noticed in how they thereafter contextualize the saying-deed.

If we ask the purposes for which they produced their gospels, several answers emerge: to provide teaching materials for new converts; to provide preaching materials for evangelism; to produce materials which could be incorporated into liturgies and services of worship; and, of course, to preserve a core of data about their "Lord."

First century readers would not approach any contemporary (to them) literature expecting historical accuracy as we might define that today. Whether they believed that everything they read or heard about a saying-deed of Jesus was "literally true" is therefore a consideration out of place historically. Had they read all three

PART TWO . . . in which I turn to the Bible

synoptics, they would have been far less concerned than are we about discrepancies, inconsistencies, even contradictions. We think differently in our era, but we must recall how they thought about such matters in theirs. The gospel writers' license to organize, collate, write, and interpret was not an issue. That they used this freedom was the normal operation in ancient literary production.

Only recent Biblical scholarship has seen the importance and taken the challenge of going "behind" the texts to look for original sayings-deeds material. It is an arduous task, with many universally demonstrable and agreed upon findings, but also with many uncertainties and unanswered questions.

Before I look at the twelve pertinent passages, I share some important conclusions at the outset. The total number of different Gehenna sayings is not eight, but five. If I discount the saying of John the Baptist, which was placed in Jesus' mouth, it is four. And four non-Gehenna "eternal fire" statements remain. One of them is a saying of the Baptist. Let me examine all of these sayings separately.

1. Matthew 5: 21–22

In this Sermon on the Mount teaching, Jesus states that calling a brother a "fool" will make one liable to the Gehenna-hell of fire. We can reasonably wonder if Jesus intended to confirm the existence of eternal torment by denouncing the use, even in extreme anger, of a word like "fool." Could such a "bad word" suddenly rise to the level of importance that one's eternal fate hinged on its utterance? We have no indication, anywhere else in scripture, that such might be the case. The verse does not appear, then, to be a didactic saying related to life after death, but a common enough warning, heard in every age: "If you say this, there are serious consequences."

Also, a quick glance at any Bible concordance will reveal how often the term, or its derivatives, is used elsewhere in the New Testament, with no thought of eternal destinies. It is even used by Jesus himself! (Matthew 7:26; 23:17, 25:2, 3, 8)

Jesus Did Not Teach Eternal Hell

I do not recall anyone who believes in eternal hell teaching that using this word is a surefire way to end there.

2-4. Matthew 5:27-30; Matthew 18:8-9; Mark 9:43-50

All three sayings contain the strangely disturbing words about cutting off or gouging out a hand, a foot or an eye. Matthew 5 omits "foot" but adds it in Matthew 18. It is, we are told, more profitable spiritually to lose these parts of one's anatomy than to be thrown into Gehenna-hell. We agree!

In Matthew 5 Gehenna is used twice. In chapter 18 it is used once, with "eternal fire" also used. In Mark 9 Gehenna is written three times in the one passage, the sum total of its usage in the entire gospel.

Suggesting bodily mutilation is in no way Jesus' actual intent. And he did not employ these grotesque pictures and images to then indirectly establish the reality of the eternally punishing realm of hell. Using such language for that purpose would be truly bizarre under any circumstances, particularly by the Nazarene teacher.

Furthermore, though this passage appears three times in the gospels, no doubt attesting to its curious importance in the first century, Jesus most often declares that the origin of human sin is clearly "the heart." To say it is the hand or eye or leg is to comment on physical ways sin might be committed.

In Mark 9:43-50, the threefold use of Gehenna-hell is followed in some manuscripts by a threefold repetition, "where their worm does not die and the fire is not quenched." If worm refers to persons, their souls, essences, kernel selves, Jesus has not used the term in a similar way elsewhere. Additionally, the verse about a never-dying worm is a quotation from Isaiah 66:24. There the language refers to the slain bodies of those who fought against the Lord. Perhaps the best translation speaks of the worms which do not die while they devour the bodies of the slain. The worms are not the dead/slain persons!

PART TWO . . . in which I turn to the Bible

    I think Jesus would not pronounce about unending torment using Old Testament texts which have nothing to do with eternity, hell, or unending punishment.

    It is true that Jesus quoted from Psalm 22 while hanging on the cross. Psalm 22:6 states, "I am a worm and not a man." That citation is about the abject humility before God of a man scorned and despised by all. It has nothing to do with anything eternal.

    Interestingly enough, following this threefold use of Gehenna, Mark writes two verses about salt and fire. Verse 49: "Everyone will be salted with fire." If Jesus means only that we will all suffer trial, temptation and pain in this life, it was hardly worth stating. That awareness is quite obviously the case. If he means that he himself will be the source and cause of life's difficulties, that is another matter. He did say in Luke 12:49, "I have come to bring fire on the earth. . ." Later, the Hebrews writer gives a connection between Jesus and God when he pens, "God is a consuming fire" (12:29). He is quoting Deuteronomy 4:24.

    The unqualified reference to "everyone" (verse 49) being salted with fire sounds like some sort of cleansing or disciplinary process. This thought is, of course, in line with my views on the nature of the "hell" that awaits us all as we are prepared by God to enter her eternal presence. (See essays which follow). Fire as something touching humans in any way is not pleasant. Neither is the cleansing and removal of one's sin. It all fits together quite well, though Mark would not likely know of this kind of thinking. I am certain, however, that Jesus knew.

    Some of Jesus' sayings are so ambiguous that they cannot be definitively and exhaustively interpreted. When we come to his "fire" utterances, we are in even denser fog. It is not particularly helpful here to analyze the usage of fire—to destroy, purify, cleanse, punish. Many outcomes from the application of fire are quite positive, despite its initial ominous potentials. Fire used to punish eternally produces images of unspeakable horror and revulsion. Fire hurts!

5. Matthew 7:19

One must recall the preaching of John the Baptist in Matthew 3:10 where the exact language is used by John: "Every tree that does not bear good fruit is cut down and thrown into the fire." This is an obvious case of a "John saying"—there are two—being placed in the mouth of Jesus by the Matthew editors. Jesus could certainly have said it, with many in the audience recalling the original utterance of John. If so, there is no evidence here that Jesus is doing anything other than quoting the strange one who "cried in the wilderness." It is not proof at all of Jesus' belief in a literal eternal hell. Had Jesus wanted to say that bad trees are really people who will "go to hell," he could easily have done so without quoting John.

Footnote: Luke 6:43-45

A significant and interesting difference is noted between Matthew 7:15-20 and Luke 6:43-45. The passages are doubtless from a common source, and contain preaching comments from John the Baptist (Matthew 3:10; Luke 3:9). In Matthew, Jesus says the tree that does not bear fruit is cut down and thrown into the fire (no Gehenna-hell). In Luke, the saying is radically modified to refer the trees to people who do good or bad out of "the heart." Luke has no one being tossed into the fire or into torment. His interest is in the quality of the inner person. Typically, Matthew's scribes have another interest, that of separating people into the righteous and the unrighteous, with accompanying rewards and punishments. Jesus did not bracket people into separate groups, such as good or evil. Many verses attest to this fact.

6-7. Matthew 10:28; Luke 12:4-5

Jesus is said to warn that everyone should fear Him who can destroy both body and soul in Gehenna-hell. It is entirely consistent with my views for Jesus to have used Gehenna-hell sayings to pronounce the direst warnings, without thereby literalizing the

PART TWO . . . in which I turn to the Bible

existence of a fiery, eternal domain. I think this is the gist of the verse.

However, the words propose an important, even shocking, question: does God have the power and the right to cast his creatures into an unending torment? Jesus surely meant it to be a jarring, sobering thought, conveying the utter seriousness and ethical rigor demanded of life in the kingdom of God.

The words, I think, relate to the ancient phrase, "the fear of the Lord." It is a reminder of the awe-filled obedience required from the "One with whom we have to do," the Lord God. We do not have shallow, casual relations with this God, whose holy power extends to this life and beyond. Fortunately for all her creatures, however, it is power defined by love, not love defined by power.

Interestingly, Jesus did not say that God will cast anyone into Gehenna-hell, nor that he had done so in the past. Still, the gripping caution is real enough for anyone who will hear.

It is worth noting that even after this stunning verse, Matthew's editors curiously add verse 29 about no sparrow falling without knowledge of "your Father." Verse 30 reassures that the very hairs of your head are numbered. Then, verse 31 gently encourages, "So do not be afraid; you are worth more than many sparrows."

The contrast between a God who damns eternally and one who lovingly watches over each and every one of her creatures could not be more stark. The contrast between going to hell and abiding in God's grace is more than telling. The contrast is between "fear" and "do not fear" is strikingly significant. God can do this or that. But in this moment God is providing daily loving care for her creatures. Had Jesus chosen to picture souls suffering in Gehenna—sent there by God—or to declare that some standing around him were undoubtedly going to be cast there forevermore, this saying would have given the perfect springboard for such a message.

8. Matthew 13:36–43

These verses relate to what purports to be Jesus' interpretation of the Parable of the Weeds. Many scholars believe that a parable is intended to make a single point, not for every word or phrase to be interpreted independently of that one main point. Almost all scholars acknowledge that Jesus spoke in parables, but few believe he provided their interpretation, as found here. It can be doubted that Jesus secreted his disciples away to tell them what such utterances "really meant."

But even if he did, as Matthew's redactors write here, the interpretation of this parable is highly problematic. Jesus' words turn the parable into an allegory full of new meaning. What Jesus explains to the disciples is clearly not what was heard previously, just moments before, by the crowds!

Both text and interpretation "don't work" agriculturally. When it comes to wheat, one does not gather the weeds before harvesting. Removing that chaff is the purpose of the threshing floor, not field hands pulling weeds one by one from thickly-planted grain. John the Baptist knew this very well (Matthew 3:12), even if Matthew did not. Jesus, in other places, displayed sound knowledge of basic farming principles, and would not likely have made these plainly naïve statements. In any event, the parable and the interpretation cannot be fully harmonized in any meaningful way.

9. Matthew 13:47–50

Matthew 13 contains eight parables. It appears that Jesus told three of them to the disciples without an audience present: Hidden Treasure, Pearl of Great Value, and the Fisherman's Net. In this privacy, Jesus explains the Parables of the Weeds and of the Net, the two dealing with eternal exclusion. We have reviewed the first of these.

Regarding the Net, the explanation again expands the story into an allegory. Verse 47 reads: "the kingdom of heaven is like a net... which caught all kinds of fish." The good fish are collected in baskets. The bad are thrown away. Verse 49 declares that the story is "really about" angels separating the wicked from the righteous, throwing those unrighteous into the fiery furnace to weep and gnash teeth.

Since I declare that Jesus did not teach eternal torment, I can easily propose a solution completely in line with universal redemption. Verses 47 and 48 may well be authentic utterances of Jesus. God's net does, indeed, bring in "all kinds of fish." But Matthew's editors have not felt that such language was in concert with the real teaching of Jesus. They add that all the bad creatures will not correctly be tossed back into the sea, the natural place for any unwanted catch. They, rather, will be consigned to the horrors of the torture chamber called hell. Fish and other sea creatures are wrongly turned into living persons sent straightaway to eternal suffering. This interpretation belongs to Matthew, not to Jesus.

Had Jesus truly intended to "teach" about heaven and hell, is it probable that he would have given this momentous inside information to his simple disciples couched in language we read here? And is it likely that Jesus would have recited a parable, and in the next breath declared its interpretation, which is plainly different from what the disciples had just heard? Why use a parable to teach what could only be labeled a cardinal principle of faith when non-figurative language would have been far more effective? In other words, why not declare this teaching openly if it is indeed about the eternal destiny of the human race? This whole scene is strangely curious if it is anything.

10. Matthew 23:15

I have always believed this to be an authentic utterance from Jesus, since it is so pointed in its scathing criticism of the Pharisees. They claimed to be the "true teachers" of Israel, and did have the ear of the populace. As such they had unchallenged opportunity to proclaim the love of God, and encourage Israel to live out its God-intended role to bless all nations. They failed miserably in this nurturing role. We know that Jesus was very hard on persons in authority over the little and the least, demanding that they minister and aid, not lord it over or exploit.

In this passage, Gehenna-hell is powerfully used, with no intention of positing the existence of eternal hell, but to chastise and chasten the ineffective "teachers." They make a convert who then becomes "twice the son of Gehenna." This is clearly a figurative, metaphorical word play—once a disciple, twice the son—making the point that conversion under the Pharisees may not lead one to godly living. If one throws one's lot in with the "sons of hell," what can one expect?

11. Matthew 23:33

This is an original saying of John the Baptist, from chapter 3:7. For the second time, Matthew's scribes place John's words in the mouth of Jesus. They make a significant change in this utterance, however. John does not use Gehenna-hell in his preaching, but Matthew's editors place the Greek word in Jesus' mouth, nonetheless.

Since this is the last Gehenna-hell saying in the gospel, perhaps Matthew's writers could not locate another such Jesus saying in their material. Even so, Jesus did not need to quote John the Baptist in order to call the Pharisees "snakes and a brood of vipers." He reckoned them arrogant and unrepentant sinners. This opinion could give him latitude to add that their lifestyle might lead them straight to the Gehenna-hell that they talked about with such relish, and which was a major tenet of their teaching. "How will you escape. . ." the ultimate implication of your own teaching that certain such sinners go to hell! Reminding them to remember their own words is in no way accepting their views on the matter.

Footnote: Comments on Matthew 24, Luke 21, and Mark 13

Before I look at the passages in Matthew 24, a few notes are necessary here. Scholars agree that Luke and Matthew had access to

PART TWO . . . in which I turn to the Bible

Mark's gospel during the writing of their lives of Jesus. Synoptic study shows that these two later editors expanded and reworked Mark's material from his chapter 13. The interesting line, "Let the reader understand," appears in Matthew and Mark. It attests to the busy concern of the editors and redactors to present, to them, very important teaching. Truly, we wish the reader could understand these challenging verses. Alas, we cannot. Even the most ardent fundamentalists cannot agree on the meaning of these lengthy sections. No one can point to any event in modern or ancient history which was described or foretold here.

The passages on the so-called Second Coming are extremely vague. All three gospels refer to the Son of Man "coming back to earth on the clouds." This appears to be quoted from Daniel 7. Matthew actually uses the name Daniel in 24:15. But if the writers are quoting Daniel 7:13, they have completely reversed its meaning. Daniel sees "One like a Son of Man coming with the clouds of heaven. He came to the Ancient of Days and was presented before him." This verse is clearly about the Son of Man ascending into heaven, not descending to the earth! The writers have misunderstood completely, and have thereby foisted this misinterpretation on the Christian community for centuries.

These verses are pure creative editorship and of very little value from a historical point of view. They play no role in Jesus' larger vision of a coming reign of sovereign love.

Footnote: Matthew 24:51

This is a Matthew parable, one of several in chapters 24 and 25, with the all too familiar theme of being ready for the return of the master or bridegroom. Matthew 24 is a hodge-podge of sayings with a very unclear narrative. Any attempt at detailing a chronology for the various events described is doomed to failure. The only safe takeaway is the admonition to watch, be ready and prepared.

The sadistic servant of verse 51 is met by the returning master with a frightful response. He is cut in pieces and assigned to a place with hypocrites, where, again, the outcasts weep and gnash their teeth. Apparently the cutting in pieces is not fatal, for the sentence is immediate ostracization.

There are other scholarly interpretations of the cutting, but the point is that the unpreparedness has dire consequences, especially if one has misused or abused one's resources, or, worse, misused other human beings.

The painful outcome for this servant is the equivalent of that for the ill-clad wedding guest in chapter 22. However, since in Matthew other "legal" sentences are handed down to other lax, poorly prepared persons, we can conclude that nothing in this passage is about eternal damnation.

12. Matthew 25:30-46

In Matthew there is a topical break between 25:30 and the rest of the book. Verse 30 ends the Parable of the Talents, as verse 31 begins the long section often titled "The Last Judgment."

Here in verse 30 we note the familiar themes of reckoning for unfaithful waiting and misuse of talents. The servant who hid his one talent was shamed and has his talent given to the wise investor who began with ten. The servant is accordingly labeled "worthless" and is predictably thrown "outside, into darkness," where he will weep and grind his teeth. He is thereby excluded from the rewards received by the others who were invited to "come and share your master's happiness" (Verses 21,23).

This subject has been presented numerous times by Matthew, with the same conclusions and outcomes. Watch, prepare, use your gifts wisely, and be rewarded. Otherwise, be rejected and suffer the painful consequences. There is no Gehenna-hell in this passage, nor in the rest of the gospel. Eternal perdition is not the teaching of the parable. Other themes predominate.

These early verses, 31-46, have been labeled a parable. If so, interpreters need not dissect each meaning. It does not matter whether they are or are not a parable, however. Salient features of this Matthew work demand our attention.

PART TWO . . . in which I turn to the Bible

1. The "righteous" are rewarded for "works," not for content-based faith.
2. The righteous have no idea that their works are for and unto the "Lord." God approves those who accomplish her will and intention even if these persons do not know her as God. This is strange teaching for Matthew.
3. The works applauded are the most basic acts of human compassion and concern now shockingly elevated to the status of criteria for determining eternal destinies.
4. The term Gehenna-hell is not used for "eternal fire" or "eternal punishment." (v. 41,46)
5. The "Son of Man" in verse 31 describes himself as "King" in verses 34 and 40, the only such self-ascriptions by Jesus in the synoptics.
6. The scene is, of course, a Second Coming scene, with an accompanying Judgment Day. Jesus appears as the Judge hearing the testimony from both the righteous and the unrighteous.
7. Before the "trial," however, the verdict is set, for the Son of Man has already separated "the sheep from the goats." (v. 32)
8. Nowhere else in the gospels does Jesus separate human beings into sheep and goats. Matthew does here, which matches his "us" versus "them" theology, one Jesus does not endorse.
9. The faith of the righteous can be defined as doing good without knowledge, deeds done ostensibly out of the simple milk of human kindness. The rewards of the King are extravagant.
10. The King, however, will summarily damn to eternal fire those who do not see the human need and respond to it, regardless of who is defined as needy.
11. If this Judgment scene is a cross section of God's dealing with the "sins of the world," it presents a very small swath of the multitudes of sin written about by Matthew. Of all the socially impactful sins that could be mentioned, Matthew strangely describes only these omitted acts of kindness.

12. If Jesus did indeed divide the human race as described here, it is quite notable that earlier in his ministry he spent a great deal of time among the "goats," rank sinners. Many of them, he implied, were faithful and good.

13. There is absolutely no mention here of anyone accepting or rejecting Jesus as their "personal savior," or having acknowledged him as either King or Lord.

14. And tellingly this: before Christ appear the Gentile nations, and among these non-Jews, many are found righteous in God's sight. They enter the eternal kingdom. Here, Matthew has wandered into universalist territory even if his scribes would not admit to having even implied such a heretical, damnable notion.

15. Nevertheless, it is quite surprising, on one hand, that some of these verses emerged from Matthew's scriptorium, since they are heavily freighted with an indiscriminant agape love. Persons are being saved here that Matthew would not typically include in the heaven-bound. But at the end, as we shall see, he returns to his own comfortable portrayal of masses consigned to eternal flames.

So, we must visit two verses of concern, 25:41 and 25:46: "Depart from me, you who are cursed, into the eternal fire...," and "Then they will go away to eternal punishment." It is helpful to note what Matthew has presented in chapter 24: destruction of the temple, signs of the end, imminent persecution, the desolating sacrilege, false Messiahs, the coming of the Son of Man, and the suddenness of that coming. Matthew 25 picks up with the Parables of the Bridesmaids, the Talents, followed by this Judgment account.

Even the most creative scholarship cannot collate these variegated endtime sayings, some of which have also been scattered elsewhere in all three gospels. But this expanded Judgment scene is quintessential Matthew theology, and stands here only. The predictable outcome is already known: some few go to Heaven, the accursed go to "eternal fire prepared for the Devil and his angels." The fire is, it seems, also prepared for many others than humans!

PART TWO . . . in which I turn to the Bible

This is Jesus' last public declaration of such frightening teaching. One wonders why. After all, Matthew's chapters 26–28 contain the Last Supper, Gethsemane, Jesus' arrest, the trial before the Council, the appearance before Pilate, the conviction, the mocking, the cross, and the resurrection. Surely most of these scenes would have given grand opportunity to all and sundry, high and low, king and beggar to hear Jesus warn to flee the wrath to come— by accepting him as Lord and Savior. But not a word. The scribes fall silent.

As it stands, Matthew's Judgment depiction is one of the most unusual passages in the Bible, possibly in the corpus of human writing. It contains some of the most humanly tender and compassionate language ever penned, coupled with shocking language lacking in any human or divine concern whatsoever. If anything in this section contains original utterances of Jesus, they must be meticulously culled and reconstructed.

One thought is pertinent to our question: Did Jesus teach unending torment? In this passage Jesus strongly and personally relates to the needs and suffering of the downcast and outcast. It is a puzzlement indeed to then ask: can one so compassionately identified with the well-being of the least, the lost, the little, and the last, consign any human being to unending, fruitless suffering forever? Especially when it seems that giving a piece of bread, or a cup of water, or making a visit, might qualify one as righteous (verses 37–39). "Enter into heaven," or "Depart into hell." These two declarations in such close proximity seem almost impossible to assign to one fully integrated personality. But that person is a Matthew scribe. That person is not Jesus of Nazareth.

This is the entire catalog of Gehenna-hell and eternal torment sayings from the synoptics. And so, some summary thoughts: if Jesus did not teach eternal hell, does it automatically follow that he taught universal redemption? What other options were there?

He could have taught that there is no personal, individual life after death. That was the position of the Sadducees. Holding such a view in the first century world meant that life's focus was upon politics to maintain the status quo, through which one could

Jesus Did Not Teach Eternal Hell

accumulate power and wealth for ease of living. Everything we know about Jesus would dictate against any view that he espoused wealth and power for and in a self-centered lifestyle.

Also, there are too many verses and stories in which Jesus refers to a life in the age to come, and that as an individual person in an otherworldly context. Doubting that Jesus believed in life after death is unworthy of serious discussion.

Jesus could have taught conditional immortality. This is, of course, the view that being resurrected to obtain a heavenly home is conditional upon one's faithful life on earth. Those who live unrighteously do not meet the condition, so they are simply raised to life from soul sleep, judged, then extinguished as human beings. They will live no more forever.

Some Christian groups believe and teach this doctrine. It is a viewpoint held by a few church fathers in antiquity. While it spares God the stigma of creating and maintaining an eternal torture chamber, it does little to forward certain ideas about God. Minimally it must affirm that God does not love all creatures enough to give them eternal life. It also suggests that while God may be powerful and wise enough to effect salvation, she does not choose so to do, for whatever reason.

There are Bible verses which can be interpreted as if this doctrine were correct. All of them can, however, be interpreted in other ways which refute the teaching.

I think we are left, then, with this: Jesus did not believe in soul sleep or eternal extinction. He did not believe in nor teach eternal hell. It seems conclusive to me that he did, therefore, believe in and teach universal salvation through God's agape love. Modern scholarship can show and demonstrate that many Gehenna-hell verses were not spoken by Jesus, or that those verses can be understood in new ways.

If he did use the term, he did so in an entirely different way than to affirm the odious doctrine of unending torment. In any event, the term was readily available in common parlance for use among the Jews and their spiritual leaders. Had Jesus desired to be

PART TWO . . . in which I turn to the Bible

absolutely plain and unequivocal about impending doom in a fiery hell, we must assert that he would surely have done so. He did not.

Footnote: *The Thief On The Cross (Luke 23:43)*

This verse has traditionally been interpreted thus: one thief turns to Jesus and goes to heaven; the other thief does not and goes to hell. The view cannot be sustained.

The primary issue in interpretation is this: what does Jesus believe about his own experience of life after his impending death? (This is a highly significant theological matter, far beyond the scope of these essays.) Then, to what otherworldly context or environment is Jesus inviting the man? What does "Paradise" mean? Is it traditional heaven? Why does Jesus use this ambiguous, even odd term? It is found only three times in the New Testament: here, 2 Corinthians 12:4, and Revelation 2:7. Old Testament usages are many. But comparing Jesus' use with 2 Corinthians and Revelation is not particularly helpful either.

Paradise suggests the more visual, aesthetic, sensual characteristics of the afterlife: gardens, trees, rivers, streets, gem stones, etc. It deemphasizes the overarching presence of God. Perhaps a thief might welcome those mental images rather than one announcing an imminent meeting with his Maker God.

Jesus would believe that everyone at death enters the presence of God. Both thieves will do that. Jesus may be implying here that the comfort in this tragic scenario is that he and the thief will find themselves in a world of love, where God will assuredly direct the next steps for both of them. He would certainly not deny that to the other thief, with whom he is not conversing. All three dead men will find themselves in utter dependence upon God, Jesus being confident that God will deal with each of them in her own wise, powerful, and loving way.

This verse does not commend a last minute repentance that leads to death and glory. We cannot imagine that at his last breath the thief will be able to sit next to Jesus in heaven! Such a view cheapens everything Christian faith has taught about answering for one's deeds on the so-called Judgment Day.

"Being with Jesus in Paradise" says absolutely nothing about the ultimate redemptive work of God in this thief's life, or in any life, in the next world. The verses powerfully demonstrate Jesus showing God's agape love to the outcast, and the least. On the cross, he ends his ministry as he had begun it—claiming everyone for the God of agape love. The story therefore portends very good news for all sinners, regardless of their end-of-life condition.

In order to believe the traditional, historical interpretation of this story, we are asked to endorse something like this: Jesus asks forgiveness for the taunting, jeering crowd of civilians and soldiers, but not for the tragic, pathetic man dying on the cross on his left. Such a view is an epic misrepresentation of a rather transparent story, and an egregious misreading of the heart of Jesus.

Footnote: The Sin Against The Holy Spirit

For centuries men and women have shuddered as they asked, "Is it possible that I have committed, or will commit, the sin against the Holy Spirit?" They ask because in each synoptic Jesus is reported as having spoken to this issue in the most ominous terms. For our purposes here, the concern is that for much Christian theology, unforgiven sin surely means eternal torment.

Jesus did say, did he not, that the sin against the Holy Spirit will not be forgiven? (Matthew 12:30-32; Mark 3:28-30; Luke 12:8-10). The exact wording seems to be that "blasphemy" against the Spirit is not forgiven.

The second part of the utterance is quite clear: something will not be forgiven. The first part is not at all clear: What is this sin? How is it defined? How committed? Much theological thought and writers' ink have gone into answering this question. But exact definitions of the "sin" and how it is committed, have not been satisfactorily or convincingly brought forth. That fact, however, does not give spiritual leeway to disregard the text. Additionally,

PART TWO . . . in which I turn to the Bible

we need not dismiss the words because the gospel writers place them in three different contexts. They are still there!

We can likely agree that the teaching is probably about impenitence, defiance, and resistance to the call, solicitation, or pleading of the Spirit. We sin when we account that spiritual invitation as of no importance, and we thrust it away from our hearts and consciences with impunity. We have grieved and blasphemed the Holy Spirit of God in that process. We have spurned the gracious and loving presentment.

If this is a correct interpretation, my question is this: when can God forgive one who refuses the offer of forgiveness and salvation? When in time and eternity?

My more complete thinking on this appears in selected essays throughout. I maintain that God can and will overcome all resistance to her proffered grace and love, and that all sinners will be saved. If that is accurate, God will, in eternity, be quite capable of dealing with the so-called sin against the Holy Spirit. But only in eternity can the sin be forgiven, for only in eternity will the sinner willingly acknowledge the sin and turn from it. This doing is God's affair, but it will be accomplished through God's loving "persuasion."

These are my concluding thoughts. God has decreed, from the foundation of the world, the salvation of all persons. God has accounted all persons righteous in Jesus Christ (Romans, passim). There is, therefore, no sin that is "unforgiveable," though some sins are obviously unforgiven at the time of one's death. Universal redemption is God's aim, and the process extends from time into eternity. God will be as active in the world to come, as he is active in this world, in bringing her sons and daughters to glory.

Jesus' words of caution ring true even as they appear enigmatic. The caution here is not a light-hearted matter, but as serious as any utterance recorded in the gospels.

Finally, I have this thought. In other passages in scripture, the term "hardness (or hardening) of the heart" appears. Initially, this act is the volitional, self-determined act of rejecting the things of God. Biblical warnings are plain: this misdirection of one's life can become "irreversible." It is a common phrase that someone has "no feeling for others, no concern, no empathy." Surely there is a mental health diagnosis for sociopaths and psychopaths. That is another issue.

Do persons in their stubborn recalcitrance ever get beyond the loving reach and eternal claim of God? Even if in moments of sinful despair or fist-pounding rage, a person may profess a complete lack of desire to "see God," he or she will not be abandoned by God, but in time saved by God. This entire book has been written to make that point!

Footnote: The Rich Man and Lazarus

Reference must surely be made to Luke's words in 16:19–31, where Jesus tells the story of the Rich Man and Lazarus. The debate rages on about whether this is, in fact, a parable. Jesus does not say. In any event, the story is placed in the context of a Jesus Sadducee confrontation. Its teaching should be viewed entirely in that light. Those issues are not a concern here, however.

But these points are pertinent. One, this is not an effort on Jesus' part to inform anyone about the geography of the afterlife, in which the Sadducees did not happen to believe. Jesus is raising other issues for their smug consideration.

Secondly, one can make a provocative interpretive case that the Rich Man in "torment" has actually begun spiritual rehabilitation through the severe mercy of pain. He can now see that the tragic outcome of his life is a consequence of his selfish, loveless disregard for many things, including the needy neighbor right at his front doorstep. Even if he cannot cross the "great gulf," he has understood the profound error of his heartless ways.

I have affirmed in these pages that a newly-defined hell has that exact redemptive purpose. Of course, the writer of Luke would not find my analysis helpful in any way. Jesus would, however.

Should a man experiencing such profound and moving repentance then be told that it is too late, and that the fires of hell will scorch him forever?

PART TWO . . . in which I turn to the Bible

That "Father Abraham" is tasked to explain the consequences of his behavior is priceless enough. Could not Luke allow the Lord God to be center stage in this sad and woeful conversation? Admittedly that scenario would then appear ungodlike, even tasteless. If this is a word from God, the thankless work will be accomplished by an intermediary. We must be struck by the kindness of Abraham's words, even if he speaks for the God who stokes the fires!

Nothing in this story has the intention of literalizing anything at all related to life to come.

Footnote: Why Bother If We Cannot Know?

In this essay I have stated that we cannot know "for certain" what Jesus said or what he did. Then why do I write at length in an attempt to demonstrate what he did not say? It is a fair question in every respect.

By saying what I do, I am joining the multitude of Biblical interpreters who declare that we have little access to what has come to be called "the historical Jesus." We know that a "gospel" is a literary genre arising within a community of believers in the unique status of Jesus of Nazareth. That fact alone has led to the appropriate question: because of their faith content, are the gospels historically reliable? That question is asked of the sheer facticity of what is presented about Jesus. Some few facts about his life can be verified independently of the gospel accounts. Most simply cannot.

Do we discount Biblical records because we have no secondary validation of what they proclaim? Not necessarily. However, do we take the position that something is true simply because it is "in the Bible?" I have said that position is self-authentification, a circular argument lacking basic logic. It is not at all persuasive and counts for almost nothing. Despite that, Christian history is filled with religious leaders who have basically claimed that it is spiritually virtuous and meritorious to believe "what the Bible says," even if what is to be affirmed may be contrary to reason or rational consideration.

Jesus Did Not Teach Eternal Hell

Our concern here is what to affirm about the life and teachings of Jesus. What, indeed, are the sources from which we can draw conclusions about his sayings and his deeds? Many scholars have spent entire lifetimes attempting to answer that. A few have concluded that the gospels are entirely valueless as historical documents. Most have agreed, however, that there is a core of data about Jesus, which can be extracted using modern tools of Biblical study. Even then, there is considerable disagreement about the content of that data. How, then does one decide? Unfortunately, the answer is this: each reader, interpreter, and scholar must carefully analyze his or her presuppositions while approaching the text, do one's best interpreting, and decide for one's self. Comparing ideas and outcomes with others is, of course, part of the process.

Most scholars can list and outline what they believe are the signal events and the authentic sayings-deeds of Jesus. There is, however, every reason to believe that this rigorous study will never produce unanimity in outcome, and that the effort will go on interminably. Such is scholarship in every field of learning and endeavor.

In this book I have spent very little time on Jesus' deeds, focusing almost entirely on sayings—those relating to eternal hell. For understanding those sayings I have relied on certain Old Testament teachings about God, which declare her love for creation and creatures. I believe that Jesus embraced that thinking and lived out the implications from it in his day-to-day life and dealings with others. In and of itself his understanding would preclude the existence of an eternal hell and of creatures actually going there under any circumstances.

I have relied primarily, however, on the epistles of Paul, and those other writings in which universal redemption is taught. Those writings, while largely ignoring almost all facts about Jesus' earthly life, present a relatively unified theology of the cosmic significance of that life. They assess Jesus' impact by a retrospective interpretive process, finding in him the perfect exemplar of God's eternal desire to show an all-inclusive eternal love to all people.

PART TWO . . . in which I turn to the Bible

We wish these New Testament scribes and writers had spent more time reflecting on the sayings and deeds of Jesus. They did not. How then did they reach their conclusions about endtime matters and the fate of persons? Clearly by means other than by believing there were "sacred materials" abroad in which Jesus taught unending torment.

We simply cannot explain why these latter day interpreters of Jesus' life would posit a universal redemption in his name if, in fact, he had not taught it. There would have been nothing unique about a first-century itinerant preacher teaching the doctrine of eternal hell. That one would appear proclaiming the stunning notion of universal salvation, through God's agape love, would have been both extraordinary and revolutionary. That seems to be exactly what occurred, and is therefore, I believe, historical fact.

PART THREE

...in which I redefine Hell

We All Go To Hell

It would seem incontrovertible that the word "hell" is beyond unfortunate for my purposes, even as it is likely impossible that I could coin a new term for our lexicon. If "hell" has to do, we can take minimal comfort in recognizing a few things about it. In some religious traditions, hell is simply a place where the dead reside, without reference to pain or suffering. Our modern word is derived from an Old English term that refers to the mysterious, shady world occupied by the dead, apparently never referencing their anguish. That is better.

In any event, a new definition of hell as "the realm of the dead" is required for my purposes. The new concept, however, must include the positing of many such realms. Why? Because despite any spiritual progress, none will be ready for that ultimate blessed heavenly abode until they have rid themselves of the baggage of every single sin. And because every single sinner is uniquely different, and therefore God knows where each needs to be in order to be rid of that sin.

All of this I affirm to be the case because God will, in short, allow no sin into her "final heaven." God can surely create the perfect environments and contexts wherein she accomplishes her saving goals of guiding each person through the process of ultimate sanctification producing holiness. God lovingly directs it all, every step of the way.

In order "to go to heaven" then, everyone must "go to hell." I am confident enough of this fact that in the coming essays I am

PART THREE . . . in which I redefine Hell

presenting a tentative itinerary for us all as we, through grace, navigate our way from hell to heaven. There is no set chronological order here, I say again. All these things must be accomplished nevertheless, and God will surely do it.

The story has been told numerous times of the young candidate for ordination in the Reformed Tradition, appearing before a stern ecclesiastical body, and being asked in stone-faced seriousness, "Are you willing to be damned for the glory of God?" The correct answer, if one desired ministerial credentials, was, of course, "Yes!"

We must not judge too harshly our religious forebears, for it was a legitimate question given their cramped and rigid ideological presuppositions. Thankfully, recent generations have been freed from such thinking through advances in scientific, philosophical, and theological understanding. That many times asked question now appears to us as very misguided in its ideas of personal devotion to a holy God, and its ideas about the purpose and plan for hell where, in their query, one who is damned would reside forevermore.

If the question to the ordinand is rephrased, "Are you willing to go to a hell in which God lovingly prepares you for unimaginable joy and bliss?," the answer should now be an unequivocal, "Yes!" Whatever God has in mind in order to procure our ultimate redemption, must be deemed an act of agape love, and must accordingly be embraced with gratitude.

Hell Is God's Hell

ACCORDING TO THE AUTHORS of several Old and New Testament books, everything exists in a purposeful relationship to its creator, God. Humans have severly limited access to that purpose, generally speaking. The fact is that most of micro- and macro- creation, with all its innumerable "parts," will never come within the orbit of human consciousness, knowledge, or reflection. For example, any observer of the night skies can well believe that astronomers are correct to predict that there are millions of galaxies. Most people who have ever lived, and most living now, have no relationship whatsoever to that fact. When one asks the "purpose" of such an extravagant, excessive creation, one can only reflect on ancient Hebrew words that such worlds give God glory, with all that is meant by that phrase. Or, one can recall the Creation Story where God labels all this vastness "Good." It seems that God is pleased by such things, and rejoices in their existence. We will never "see" even a small portion of the wonders of the cosmos. God, it seems, "sees" them and delights in what he sees.

If all things exist for God, what is the purpose of hell, however it is defined? What is its relationship to God in the role and function of accomplishing the will of God, however mysterious? Since it is proclaimed by many Christians that vast numbers of human beings will be going to a fiery hell forever, we can surely speculate boldly about such things. We will do that now.

It appears to be the case that in most theological literature about eternal hell, God is presented as if the classic doctrine of

PART THREE . . . in which I redefine Hell

Deism were completely correct. That is, God creates that hell, withdraws, then "watches" to see how it will play out. Adhering to this view is quite understandable at one level, for we all have a severe visceral reaction to the idea and notion that God is an active player in the things transpiring in a place of unending torment. Theologians have no difficulty affirming that God is very much involved in the ongoing life of the church, performing miracles, giving gifts, directing hearts, answering prayers. The same is often said about God's doings among the throngs in heaven, where, apparently, God lives! But can God sincerely be thought of as having "hands on" control of any part of the life and operation of everlasting hell fire? The thought is unacceptable, but the thought is simply unavoidable. The God of Deism is the only God which can be emotionally tolerated and allowed into human consciousness; a God far, far away, doing anything but directly overseeing and orchestrating the suffering of millions.

Regardless of one's ideas about God, however, if hell is everlasting, tormenting, dead end, with no prospect of anything ever being different, then the purpose of that hell is extremely clear. It exists to punish and inflict pain. God's role appears to be purely managerial, not salvational. God, while cognizant of the horrible suffering of her creatures, is impassive at best. He is uninfluenced by the plight of his creatures. And it must be concluded that God is eternally satisfied, even pleased, with the purpose and role of this hell!

Martin Luther, the genius of the Protestant Reformation, is said to have stated, "The devil is God's devil." I have no interest in bringing the devil into these essays, but Luther's thinking is equally exact and suggestive for our topic. I can say it thus: Hell is God's hell, if that hell is rightly defined. Hell is God's hell if God is love.

Why does hell exist? As an environment in which God begins the eternal salvation of the human race. Its goal is part and parcel of everything God has done in order to redeem all persons. It is an essential component in that monumental undertaking of grace and mercy. It is a place of God's own creation, and it exists for God. If hell is God's hell, and it most assuredly is, and if hell is a context for saving and redeeming, and it most assuredly is, then the astonishing fact is inescapable: wherever else God is, God must also be in hell!

Footnote: Eternal Forgiveness

In the next two essays I offer tentative and suggestive ideas for how God may lovingly interact with individuals as she brings each one to the point at which she utters, "Enter into eternal rest." The following points must be kept firmly in mind as interpretive introduction to the coming essays.

One: God knew, before creation, that the human race would sin.

Two: God lovingly forgave the entire race of all its sin, even before creation.

Three: This is clearly articulated in several Old Testament texts, and supremely presented in the writings of the Apostle Paul, especially the Book of Romans.

Four: The unique one, Jesus of Nazareth, showed that indiscriminate, all-inclusive forgiveness to everyone. His life is a literal fulfillment of God's "desire of the ages" to claim and to incorporate all her children into a coming realm of agape love.

Five: God's forgiveness is from eternity, and therefore not dependent upon anyone meeting humanly-devised criteria in order to qualify for that forgiveness.

Six: God's cosmic decisions must be personalized in the life of each individual, beginning in this world but unavoidably continuing into the worlds to come.

Seven: In order for God's saving activity to be eternally accomplished, each individual must appropriate it by coming to understand and to acknowledge "that from which they are being saved," that is, the gravity and depravity of their own sin, and personal entanglement in sin.

PART THREE . . . in which I redefine Hell

Eight: God alone can save. She must usher each individual through the disciplinary process leading to the change she demands and requires. This must include both pain and joy by definition.

Nine: All speculations about God's means and methods for accomplishing all of this are beyond our knowing and completely mysterious. We have no revelation about these details.

Ten: Since we will all go through this process, early or late, we do well to take heed to "how we live our lives."

Eleven: God's desire is a freewill worshipful and loving response to her solicitations toward holiness. One of the greatest mysteries of life in the age to come will be the out-working of this process in every individual.

The following two essays contemplate that process of individual appropriation of the purifying work of God in order to attain the eternal salvation already announced, promised, and arranged by a loving God.

What In Hell Is Going On? Resistance and Renewal

IF HELL IS GOD'S hell, designed to implement God's saving purposes, what actually happens in hell to accomplish those ends? Since everyone needs spiritual refinement as they progress toward perfection and holiness, God must clearly accomplish several things in this intermediate state. In this essay I address two of these essential functions of hell: God must overcome each sinner's resistance, and God must completely reform the sinner.

Some ancient Christians are said to have welcomed death for many reasons, one of which was stated thus: "We embrace death because thereby we cannot sin anymore." Were they correct? I believe the answer comes down to how one defines the act of sinning. Is it the same volitional action, in the world to come, as we have defined that action in this world below? It seems certain that it cannot be so. There are vast differences in the definition and description of any sin which could be committed in any realm beyond this one. The caveat is, however, that there is absolutely no sin to be committed in the final heaven of God.

These are my speculations.

One, the idea of "corporate" sin will vanish in the next world. Institutional forms of sin manifest themselves beyond the level of individual sin, and they take on a life of their own. We are all familiar with the reality of transpersonal sin in economic and political systems, in human physical and mental conditions, in accumulated environmental neglect, in written law, in religious

PART THREE . . . in which I redefine Hell

oppression, and in endemic prejudice. The list is a lengthy one and goes on. Yet, no single human being can be pointed to as the "cause," the responsible and guilty party, for these terrible realities which are a blight on the planet and on the lives of millions.

I think it quite safe to say that corporate—institutional sin cannot transfer its evil power to any realm controlled by God's love. This sin will, thankfully, be no more.

Second, I am convinced that in an age beyond this one, persons will not be able to sin against other persons. I am persuaded that God will not allow abuse, injury, bullying, condescension, ridicule, shaming, etc. No one will be able to harm the neighbor, the other, protected now by Almighty God.

Third, so what sin is left for persons to "commit" in the presence of God? I struggle for the term, but in the end I define it as "resistance." Whatever else sin is, it is human resistance to accepting the establishment of the realm of God's love, including every attribute and characteristic of that realm incorporated into the lives of its "citizens." It is, therefore, the loving function and task of God to overcome that resistance in order to bring everyone into that kingdom which has no end. Who else but God can do it!

By Biblical definition, all sin is against God. Granting that in every case, perhaps a further delineation is helpful here. In this world we can sin directly against others and indirectly against God. We can reverse that, of course, and sin directly against God and indirectly against others. It seems worth considering that in any world to come, we will display our sinful selves only this way: directly against God. All institutional-corporate sin is gone. All human-to-human sin is gone. It is only the individual sinner in an encounter with the thrice-holy God in a realm before God's final heaven. The states are raised frighteningly and exponentially!

I have no ability to predict how long it will take for the most recalcitrant sinner to acquiesce to the purifying power of God's love. I have no idea how God plans to expose sinners to the awe of her holiness. In short, I have no irrefutable information on God's regimen for overcoming human resistance. It will, however, most surely be done. Here, I speculate boldly!

I do know this. It is not simply a matter of overcoming human protest or opposition. It is also a matter—in that very process—of individual spiritual reformation, integration, and transformation.

God demands that a new spiritual person emerge, one distinctively unique, as on earth, but now in the perfect "image of God." God eternally affirms the integrity of the human personality and its freewill, recreated by and through agape love, thereby maximizing its every God—intended capacity. The richness of such a community of God's redeemed is a dazzling and breathtaking prospect to consider.

But there is more for the God of love to accomplish for her beloved children in an intermediate state designed "to save."

What In Hell Is Going On?
Forgiveness and Reconciliation

IN THE PREVIOUS ESSAY, I again affirmed that hell's fundamental goal is the sinner's perfection and holiness. To do that, God lovingly works to overcome all resistance and to effect reformation and transformation. I now advance upon that definition by introducing two other aspects of God's eternal activity: God must forgive every sin and God must orchestrate human interpersonal reconciliation. I state again that there is no set order in God's divine work. This is all God's affair, as she completes what she has begun, and has desired for all her creatures from the foundation of the world. We remember that before the creation, God foresaw it in prospect of things she knew would come to pass. That prospective forgiveness now finds its total completion. God knew that the world would be populated only by sinners and heaven populated only by the perfected.

We can affirm the most commonplace notion of all, that heaven awaits only those who are forgiven. That is certainly true as long as we do not define the act of God's forgiveness as a magical recreation of every aspect of our lives and personalities. The moment after death, how different, indeed, is the deceased? We can only imagine! But, has all resistance been shattered, every sin acknowledged and forgiven, every relationship reconciled, every deep and dark imagining of the heart eradicated? Of course not. If not, then do we suppose that God now works as a wizard with special powers who will mutate and transmorph his children

What In Hell Is Going On? Forgiveness and Reconciliation

immediately upon their deaths into some new creaturely entity? If she did that, would they be the same individual persons and personalities they were the moment before death? No. They would each be another "person" entirely.

But this kind of image is surely wrong headed, even if it is the only way to make the word "immediate" understandable in the saving process for those who believe it happens that way. It does not. This cannot be an immediate occurrence.

I can say it plainly: forgiveness of sins by the Lord God Almighty is not the only action required to perfect or prepare persons for heaven. Forgiveness of sins, even by God, though essential, is not enough. Forgiveness is a "blessed incompletion!"

I boldly state that Christians must drop any fuzzy, unhelpful definition of forgiveness by which is implied that in forgiveness everything is completed for the dead to join God and all the saints forevermore. That is magical thinking at its best, even as it disguises what everyone knows in the innermost heart: that is not all there is to it. Forgiveness of sins, without individual maturational growth to spiritual perfection, is profoundly incomplete.

Nothing happens without the individual appropriation of the already-granted eternal forgiveness of the God of love. Granted. But I propose that there is another essential step. The step must be taken by all and can be accomplished completely only in specially-prepared contexts after one's physical death. I propose that God must couple the concept of forgiveness with the concept of reconciliation.

This is a Biblical doctrine of utmost importance. There are any number of scenes of forgiveness in the New Testament. There are also numerous scenes of reconciliation. As memorable as any is the "Father Waiting for the Prodigal Son," as told by Jesus in Luke. The young man is tenderly welcomed home by the loving embrace of his happy father. The son is forgiven. Their reconciliation is also complete.

What then is left for this humble, joyful returning son? There is an elder brother who is resentful of the entire situation. What must happen now? No other word is as satisfactory here as

PART THREE . . . in which I redefine Hell

reconciliation. All with the father may be settled and complete. But forgiveness, reconciliation, and a newly-defined relationship between the brothers awaits. Will this be warm, pleasant, and effortless? It would appear to be just the opposite. Can the earthly father of the parable command the reconciliation of his sons? He can never assure its outcome. But can the heavenly Father-Mother God command it of his created ones? Command that it be done? Yes. And she does. God, it seems, has more to accomplish than simple glorious forgiveness.

In eternity we will, as is known, meet everyone we have sinned against, and with whom we have not reconciled, for whatever reason. Though forgiven and accounted righteous by God, we still have the task of reconciliation with them all. Minimally, we must genuinely encounter all (they are forgiven sinners also, with the same task as ours) against whom we have sinned, and we must eternally and lovingly achieve peace. We with them and they with us.

How does God "pull this off?" Our answers are all speculative, but not implausible. To affirm that God can create contexts, environments, and situations in which such reconciliation must occur seems perfectly reasonable. And God can do that as easily as she can create a world and a cosmos in the first place.

What is not plausible is some such idea that we will not have to deal with our interpersonal sin, that it will be closeted away, never to be remembered in eternity. That is a caricature of the concept of personal redemption, "full disclosure," an open heart, and ultimate perfection in salvation. It is totally dismissive of required reconciliation.

The New Testament, in more than one place, speaks of one's life being open and transparent on "Judgment Day." Whatever else that means, one thing is clear: we cannot sin and "get away with it." Much of that sin involves others. That our sin will be known to all is an idea which is highly disconcerting to everyone. But the truth is irrefutable: every other sinful human being will be in the same position before a merciful God. Since this is obviously the case, we will all have one more reason to worship the God who loves us enough to deal with all our secret and open sin, forgive us, and

What In Hell Is Going On? Forgiveness and Reconciliation

reconcile us—in spite of everything! Through the grace of a loving God, we can and will lovingly embrace each other.

Our comfort and reassurance in all this must reside in trusting God to "handle" it, and that to her own glory. We can be certain that God is perfectly prepared for every aspect of dealing with the matters of our sin and our interpersonal reconciliation.

"Eye has not seen, nor ear heard, nor have entered into the human heart, the things which God has prepared for those who love him." So said Paul. I will change the last phrase of that heart-pulsing promise, adding this: ". . .the things which God has prepared not only for those who love him, but also for those who are loved by God." That is everyone. Everyone loved by God, loving God, and loving each other.

Soft On Sin?

OPPONENTS OF THE DOCTRINE of universal salvation can often be heard to say that it is weak, mushy, and soft on sin. Here are some pertinent responses.

1. Sin is a solely religious—theological concept.
2. Only God can declare and communicate standards for human behavior against which one could sin.
3. Sin has no place in ideas about right and wrong in any human moral-ethical system.
4. Sin is God's affair alone, in this life and in any age to come.
5. Human ideas about how God should deal with sin are quite irrelevant.
6. Theologically, humans do not sin against other humans. Different terms must be used to describe any such action "against the other." Sin can become a term in such an interaction only in reference to God. Even then, ultimately, the sin is against God.
7. God will act in perfect accord with the divine attributes in every determination relating to the final disposition of sin.
8. The Bible clearly defines the plight of the entire human race as entanglement in sin.
9. The Bible declares all sin as an abomination in the sight of God.

10. The Bible teaches that all humans commit sins (plural), but also have a "sin nature," that is, a predisposition toward sinning. God must deal with both, which fact demands that God act in both this life and the life to come.
11. It is not "necessary" for humans to sin, but it is inevitable that they will do so.
12. Even so, God is not "shocked" by human sin, and is quite longsuffering in the reaction to it.
13. Jesus of Nazareth is said to have died on a cross to and for sin. This represents God's most intimate and "personal" involvement in human sin.
14. Old Testament ideas about God's reaction to sin must be moderated by teachings in certain portions of the New Testament.
15. Some New Testament teachings on God's reaction to sin must be discarded.
16. No sin can enter the "kingdom of heaven" in any guise or shape.
17. Advocates of a doctrine of neverending hell view that hell as a solution to Item 16, an eternal separation of good and evil.
18. Advocates of a doctrine of "conditional immortality" view that as a solution to Item 16, the eternal extinction of both sin and sinners.
19. Advocates of a doctrine of universal salvation view that as a solution to Item 16, the eternal eradication of all sin in the lives of all sinners, leaving only ultimate good.
20. Those declaring universalism soft on sin are guilty of their own accusation if their "plans of salvation" are dismissive of individual and interpersonal sin. Some declare persons eternally "saved" with no emphasis on, or demand for, a renewed, transformed life. A German theologian coined the term, "cheap grace." It is highly applicable here.

The True Harrowing Of Hell

No one has been able to definitively relate how the phrase, "He descended into hell," ended up in the Apostles Creed. Nor has there been unanimous agreement on what the line actually means. Christians have recited the sentence since the fourth century, though there have been modern believers who have refused to speak the curious words, and that for a variety of reasons.

The origin of the four words may lie in the attempt of the early church to describe what happened to Jesus between his death on the cross Friday afternoon, and his resurrection on Sunday morning. So, he descended into hell.

Scripture does state that Jesus "went and made proclamation to spirits in prison." (1 Peter 3:19). 1 Peter 4:6 says that the "gospel was preached to those who are dead." Ephesians 4:9 relates that Jesus "descended to the lower depths of the earth." There are other allusive Scripture references along similar lines.

The earliest telling of the accompanying story appears in the apocryphal "Gospel of Nicodemus," and has currency in many sermons, poems, and other writings throughout the Middle Ages. It was a favorite image in art, with numerous painters and iconographers using the topic as a theme.

The attending story is this: upon his death Christ went to the realm of the dead, Hades, not Gehenna-hell, in order to inform the not-yet-ready-for-heaven righteous that their salvation had come. Accordingly, Christ brought these righteous, from ages past, with him into the heavenly realms. This all transpired as he awaited his

The True Harrowing Of Hell

triumphant resurrection. He seems to have left the unrighteous to their deserved state and end, as apparently they would go from Hades to Gehenna-hell at the Second Coming and its looming Judgment Day.

The quaint and charming story was dubbed, "The Harrowing of Hell" late in its life cycle, "harrow" being an archaic English word for "to plunder or to rob." Hence, Christ goes to Hades in order to plunder it, to rescue the soon-to-be-saints and escort them homeward.

My interest in this important piece of early Christianity may be obvious. In it, God-through-Christ shows passion and concern for the already dead. He goes to where they are, with the message of salvation and hope. The realm of the dead is harrowed, robbed of souls destined now for a happier dwelling place. Christ accompanies them to heaven.

The intuition of those early Christians was perfectly sound: God has always maintained a loving, active interest in the dead, for they are his dead. Their exclusive particularism was not correct, however. God is interested not only in "good people" in hell, but all people there or anywhere. And God will go to unimagined lengths to reclaim, embrace, and save her beloved children.

Christian universalism has come to harrow the traditional notion and teaching, Gehenna-hell, of its frightening, devastating effect on people and cultures. This nightmare has been playing itself out for twenty centuries. It is quite impossible to humanly calculate the crushing impact on history of the idea that God is not quite loving enough to save all his creatures. Then to add that, furthermore, God has, by the way, intentionally designed and constructed an eternal hell of unimagined horrors for most of these creatures. A pall has fallen on all peoples, of all times and places, who have heard that disturbing message. It is Christianity's shame!

This brand of faith cannot be "good news," since its ominous backdrop is threat of painful terror and retribution. Therein, God's character is besmirched, belittled, and degraded to that of a petty tyrant and retaliating, revengeful "monster." Such a deity is not at all the Abba-Father-Mother-God of Jesus of Nazareth.

PART THREE . . . in which I redefine Hell

It is the historic time for a better, brighter future for the true Christian faith which universalism espouses. It is the faith of Jesus, Paul, and other New Testament disciples. This faith proclaims that God will save us all, and we can rest confidently in its comfort and hope. It is a message for all the world. God is love. Love will love for all eternity. Hell will, indeed, be emptied with a resounding shout!

Conclusion

THEOLOGY AS A TERM means "words about God." Theos means God. Logos means word. Simple enough. In early Christian theology some thinkers believed that God was so remote and distant that we could say almost nothing definitive about him. Some of today's thinkers appear to have gone to the other extreme by claiming that we can know and say an exhaustive amount about God and her activity, in both time and eternity.

The Bible, Christian theology and all its creeds must contain millions of words. But where they place humanly defined limits on the wisdom, power, and love of God, they are words used in profound error.

Despite its stunning verbal quantity, I am convinced that the language of much of Western theology is severely restrictive and confining in its definition of God. A God who damns the majority of the human race is clearly enchained in theological language derived from very rigid interpretations of the Bible. When words in certain books of scripture are forced onto all views about God, the net effect is the "linguistic creation" of a God who is too small for other words of scripture. If God is agape love, for example, then many other things declared in holy writ cannot be an accurate portrayal of God. They must be discarded as words describing views of the writers, interpreters, editors, and redactors. They are not "words about God."

I have taken a delimited approach to scripture which declares that words about God's love give the only lens through which all

PART THREE . . . in which I redefine Hell

other scripture must be read. I have said that God's character is, in fact, the true issue here. My conclusion is that God is much "bigger" than our limited vocabularies can ever describe, and that her agape love is quite boundless now and forever.

In the end, then, there are two essential theologies at work in Christian thought. One believes in a God who will not save all the human race. The other believes he will.

One day while Jesus was teaching, a group of disciples was astonished at his words, and asked an urgent question: "Who then can be saved?" Jesus' answer was quite satisfying for us at this end point of our study: "With humanity it is impossible, but with God all things are possible" (Matthew 19:26).

Those hearers were not asking the question this book has posed: "Is is possible that God will finally save everyone?" They were not asking my question, yet the answer is precisely the same: "All things are possible with God." So in terms of sheer possibility—to use Jesus' words—the answer to my question must be: "Yes. It is possible." What God can do through her power, wisdom, and love is impossible to limit.

In another context, on another day, but perfectly pertinent here, Jesus asked, "Why don't you judge for yourselves what is right?" (Luke 12:57). With reference to what a loving God can possibly do with the eternal destiny of all persons, everyone must, one way or the other, do just that!

Where To Go From Here

THOSE OF US WHO believe in universalism understand full well that the doctrine has radical implications for many, many other topics, questions, and issues in theology. I will offer a few of those topics that occur to me. Here, I will simply list the items and end this book without further comment.

1. The place and status of other world religions and of interfaith dialogue.
2. The doctrine of the "person" of Christ.
3. The doctrine of the "work" of Christ.
4. The origin of evil and the place of overwhelming human and animal suffering.
5. The status of such entities as "principalities and powers," including investigating the reality status of so-called evil beings.
6. The origin of human personal faith in God.
7. Institutionalizing the doctrine of universal redemption in a/ the "church."
8. Universalist ethics in human affairs and human conflict, especially war.
9. Exploring the New Testament Greek definitions of "eternity" and "agape."
10. Defining a social agenda for believers in universalism.
11. Ascertaining the authentic agapeistic teachings of Jesus.

PART THREE . . . in which I redefine Hell

12. Defining "sin."
13. The nature of the afterlife and human embodiment therein.
14. The New Testament terms referring to Jesus: Savior, Christ, Messiah, Lord, Son of Man, etc.
15. Questions about "the end of the world."
16. The "religion" of Jesus.
17. Jesus' concept of God.
18. The place of punishment in universalist thought.
19. Universalist interpretation of the entire Bible.
20. Articulating and resolving all social justice issues in the light of the teachings of universalist theology.
21. Universalism as the foundation for all pastoral care, ministry, and mission.

I state again that a true agapeistic universalist theology will require a revolutionary new exposition of all the items above, certainly, and thereby of every so-called doctrine in "Christian" faith. The world awaits a thoughtful presentation of these and other topics!

www.ingramcontent.com/pod-product-compliance
Lightning Source LLC
Chambersburg PA
CBHW070913160426
43193CB00011B/1441